PHILOSOPHIES & PROFUNDITIES
Common Sense in Uncommon Times

I0839975

Copyright © 2018 by Ed Nielsen

All rights reserved. No part of this book may be reproduced in any form or by any electronic or mechanical means, or the facilitation thereof, including information storage and retrieval systems, without permission in writing from the publisher, except by a reviewer, who may quote brief passages in a review. Any members of educational institutions wishing to photocopy part or all of the work for classroom use, or publishers who would like to obtain permission to include the work in an anthology should send their inquiries to Ed Nielsen, 3 Old Applewood Lane, Hendersonville, NC 28739.

Published by Ed Nielsen
Coned3@BellSouth.net
ISBN-10: 1987587979
ISBN-13: 978-1987587975
Printed in the United States of America
April 2018

OTHER BOOKS BY ED NIELSEN

Warriors, nine first-person accounts from the Vietnam War

Classical Classics, 10 essays on various aspects of classical music, plus 126 reviews of the finest recordings of the best classical music ever written

Assault on Avignon, with Gene Carman, the true story of a WWII navigator-bombardier and his crew who flew 29 missions over Italy and southern France before being shot down and captured by the Germans

Persevere, with Tony Selius, the factual account of a young boy and his family trying to survive in Nazi Germany

Softball 101, playing tips and training techniques for anyone who plays a game on a diamond, especially slowpitch softball players

Little Things Win Big Games, with Larry Gabe, a comprehensive book on the fundamentals and fine points of playing baseball (used as a text at several universities)

Cong Catchers, with Lee Halverson, the true experiences of an MP dog handler and his cohorts during the Vietnam War

For more information or to order any of the above, go to:

BooksByEdNielsen.com

This book is dedicated to my lovely bride Connie. You provide strong encouragement in all my endeavours, except those that might be questionable. In all cases I value your sage advice and companionship.

You suffered in silence as I put long hours into writing this book. When a glimmer of light finally appeared at the end of the tunnel, you provided a sanity check, making sure the manuscript wasn't too much of a mess. Any errors remaining are mine alone; you were just too overwhelmed by their sheer quantity to catch them all. If this book has any merit whatever, it's probably due in large part to your efforts.

Love always,
Ed

TABLE OF CONTENTS

INTRODUCTION

I'm an old, retired guy who has always had an interest in current events. No one tells me what to think; I've developed my own opinions and observations on many things. In this volume I've expounded on quite a few of them.

While the essays contained herein are my opinions, I've done my best to build them on a factual foundation, no wishful thinking or fantasies. My ideas aren't special, maybe no better than yours. The main difference is that I've spent some time putting my ideas on paper. Hopefully, I've managed to do it in a clear, lucid manner. I've shared some of these thoughts with friends and relatives, usually with good response. Some of these contents have even appeared in other publications.

There may be some things in here that hadn't occurred to you and will get you thinking about them. You probably won't agree with everything I have to say, but I hope you'll defend my right to say what I've said. I'd do the same for you.

Civility in disagreement is crucial. No one will agree with everything anyone has to say. After all, if two people agree on everything, one of them is unnecessary.

Everyone believes their opinions and observations are spot-on, but mine really are! I hope you enjoy reading my pontifications half as much as I've enjoyed writing them.

ON WRITING

The day I started writing this book, my older daughter called me. After we visited for a while, she said, "Boy, you're in a good mood this morning!"

I'm an upbeat kind of guy anyway, but when I'm on a writing project I get euphoric. *That's* why Angel noticed my upbeat mood. I've always admired a well-turned phrase because it's clear and requires no pause to comprehend. I do my best to produce some of my own. When I think I've done that, I feel very good about life.

I've enjoyed some of Stephen King's books because they're easy to read—he's a master of a well-turned phrase. Maybe I'm having some success in that area, too. I've had several friends tell me I wouldn't need to sign my personal letters and they'd still know it was me because I write just like I talk. A sister-in-law finished reading an essay and asked me if I had written it. When I said I had, she said, "I should have known because it reads so easy."

Those are some of the better compliments I've ever received on my writing.

I also try to be considerate of a reader's time. Before finishing a project, I go through the manuscript with a fine-tooth comb, eliminating every word, phrase, sentence, and paragraph that isn't essential. I hope you find this book to be lean meat with no fat, bone, or gristle.

ON GRAMMAR

I have a fair grasp of the subject and there are a few pet peeves I'd like to share with you.

First is the frequent confusion between *who* and *that*. For example, I've seen excellent writers put forth a sentence such as, "Robbie is the person *that* led the charge." I contend that Robbie or any other person is a *who*, not a *that*.

Another faux pas, in my humble opinion, is the redundant use of the word *why*. For example, you'll often see sentences such as, "Human nature is the reason *why* that happens." The word *why* is totally unnecessary.

I believe the word *that* may be the most overused word in the English language. For example, "I believe *that* the word that may be the most overused word in the English language." Notice I've repeated the first sentence but added an extra *that* without imparting any additional information. Notice how many times the word appears unnecessarily in other writings and avoid it in your own.

A prolific best-selling author who shall go nameless can't seem to go a paragraph without italicizing at least one word. No writing requires that much emphasis and is very distracting to the reader. In fact, too many italics will dilute their effectiveness. *What's so special about that word?* the reader will wonder, possibly going back to see what he'd missed, usually nothing. Eventually, the reader becomes immune.

Another no-no according to Professor Nielsen is the overuse of the exclamation point. That punctuation mark is meant to emphasize something, but overuse dilutes its effectiveness.

Some folks say things like, "I'm going to try *and* find a solution." Instead, they should say, "I'm going to try *to* find a solution." They're only doing one thing, so the conjunction is inappropriate.

There's a ton of confusion, or just plain misuse in my opinion, on when to use "a" and when to use "an" before words beginning with "H." Here's an example of the most blatant example of misuse: "It was *an* historic occasion." The first time I heard that it came from Howard Cosell and I cringed. It just didn't sound correct, so I looked it up and I *should* have cringed.

A word beginning with a silent "H" should be preceded by "a," not "an." For example, a historic occasion, not an historic occasion; a humble man, not an humble man; and a humorous story, not an humorous story. Conversely, it's an honest mistake, not a honest mistake; an homage to freedom, not a homage to freedom; and an honorable settlement, not a honorable settlement.

Cosell was a very bright man and if you had any doubts he would have told you he was. I wonder if he didn't start that trend just to see if he could make other people adopt it, assuming if Cosell said it that way it must be right. And, sure enough, they did. He must be grinning in his grave.

If used long enough and often enough, eventually such things become standard and accepted. As I said, my grammar book doesn't do it that way. It's an old book but I won't change my opinion even if other, newer grammar books begin to change. As I also said, it just doesn't sound right!

Commas

I'm a big fan of the "Harvard comma." Just in case you're not familiar with the term, it advocates using a comma between all items in a list of three or more. For example: James, John, and Fred are brothers. The comma following John is a Harvard comma and I think it clarifies things and makes reading much easier, one of the primary goals in my writing.

Some references, such as the *Associated Press Style Book*, disagree with me; they don't advocate using the Harvard comma. Maybe they're trying to save ink.

Here's an extreme example of how not using the Harvard comma muddies reading: "Laurel and Hardy, Abbott and Costello and Martin and Lewis are famous comedians." Just read that sentence again to see if a comma following "Costello" wouldn't make the sentence much simpler. Even if you're familiar with these comic duos, reading that sentence probably will cause you to pause to sort out what's being said. I believe the Harvard comma *always* simplifies a sentence and speeds reading comprehension. Plus, I'm utterly profligate when it comes to using ink.

Now that I've expounded on some of my pet peeves and grammatical idiosyncrasies, I'll do my best not to commit any of them in this book.

ON SPORTS

Among other definitions, my dictionary says *sport is a physical activity engaged in for pleasure*. There's also the generally understood definition about a person being a good sport. In other words, the person referred to takes pleasure in sporting activities and sees to it that other participants enjoy themselves as well. A good sport neither gloats in victory nor pouts in defeat.

Poor Sportsmanship
Many participants have lost that sense of sportsmanship, especially at the professional level. In victory, they go out of their way to boast about their own achievements and belittle those of the opposition. In defeat, they again belittle the opposition, excuse their own deficiencies, blame the officials, or become morose. Sometimes all the above.

There's an all too frequent occurrence of fans burning and looting a city when the home team loses the championship, or even when it wins! In either case, how does it make sense to burn and loot one's own neighborhood?

My first awareness of professional sports goes back to the early 1950s. I don't recall Rocky Marciano, Willie Mays, Sammy Baugh, George Mikan or any of the other athletes from that period being boastful about themselves or derisive of their opponents. They were modest about themselves and respectful of others.

So, what changed and when?

It may have begun with Cassius Clay (later named Muhammed Ali). Clay was an excellent athlete, having won the light-heavyweight boxing championship at the 1960 Olympics. Soon thereafter he turned professional. He made a huge splash with his brash boastfulness, predicting victory over his foes and even declaring in which round he'd knock them out. When that happened, he'd brag about being the greatest. He may have been the greatest—his record tends to support that—but many folks were turned off by his big mouth. I, for one, rooted against him in every bout, wanting someone to beat him so badly he'd have no choice but to be humble in defeat. I'll admit he sold a ton of tickets that way.

Clay's braggadocio quickly spread to other athletes, both professional and amateur.

But baseball players have an unspoken etiquette they usually follow. That's especially true of a player hitting a home run. After he's sure the ball is out of the park, he'll usually put his head down and trot around the bases. Some players don't do that, preferring to stand at the plate to admire their feat before swaggering around the bases. That grates on pitchers; they believe the hitter is showing them up. Back in the days of pitchers like Bob Gibson and Don Drysdale, such a hitter had better be wearing body armor the next time he came to the plate because the pitcher was going to put a fastball in the batter's ribs. Such retribution is not allowed these days, but it'd certainly put more respect back into the game if it was.

Basketball is such a fast-paced game that a player dares not pause to gloat, lest the game go past him and turn his pride into instant shame. Hockey is also a fast-paced game and players treat each other so roughly as it is; one can only imagine it getting rougher in response to unsportsmanlike conduct. Golf may be the most polite game on the planet; everyone is a gentleman or gentle lady.

Football is another story. Gridiron competitors some-times have gaps of half a minute or more between plays. That gives them time to talk trash, do end zone dances, and generally disrespect the game and their opposition. Sadly, many players never pass up such an opportunity.

One of the most flagrant such exhibitions took place in a game involving the Carolina Panthers playing at the San Francisco 49ers. The year was 2015, a season the Panthers would go on to the Super Bowl. They were undefeated late in the season, having had their way with opponents every Sunday. Panthers' quarterback Cam Newton made a nice run for a score late in the game with the outcome no longer in doubt. Newton went to the sidelines and ran along the bleachers, smiling, head cocked and hand to his ear, as if to say, *Look what I just did! Where are the cheers for me?* Newton not only disrespected the game and his opponents, he disrespected his opponents' fans as well.

Panthers' coach Ron Rivera said this about Newton's shenanigans: "I love his spirit and his enthusiasm for the game. I don't want to do anything to dampen that."

A coach needs to stick up for his players, but maybe there's a limit.

Leading up to the Super Bowl that season, Newton was nearly as brash as Clay. "They've never seen a quarterback like me," he said of his opponents, the Denver Broncos.

"They won't know what to do!"

Au contraire! Newton spent most of the game staring at the stadium ceiling instead of downfield. The Broncos sacked him numerous times, even took the ball away from him at his own goal line and scored a touchdown. Newton was chagrinned but unrepentant at the postgame press conference, stalking out without answering the first question.

I just love it when a poor sport gets humiliated.

If I were the NFL Commissioner, I'd enact a rule whereby whenever a player misbehaves as Newton did in the 49ers game, the officials would immediately signal a two-minute timeout. During that special pause, opposing players would be free to do whatever they like to the offending player, resulting in no fouls or penalties of any kind. Anyone who tried to come to the aid of the offending player would be suspended for multiple games.

I once heard Andy Rooney address the poor sportsmanship phenomenon in pro football. He declared that boorish behavior is excusable because players have never been taught better. Andy had no bigger fan than me, but he was wrong on this one. Every one of those players participated at the college, high school, and probably lower levels of the sport. Only the NFL permits such boorish behavior, finally allowing some players to display their true colors.

Getting back to Newton for a minute, early the following season an unusual protocol seemed to be in place—the NFL officials must have read my mind. Newton got creamed, hit late by defenders on many occasions. Most of those hits should have resulted in penalties and many were grounds for ejection. But the officials threw no flags. It's as if they were sending Newton a message: *Get your act together, respect the game and your opponents, and we'll start calling penalties on your tormentors.*

Newton eventually missed a few games with a concussion. When he returned, he appeared to have gotten the message and toned down his antics.

Back in the 1970s, a rookie scored a touchdown during a preseason game. He immediately performed an epileptic exhibition in the end zone. When he got to the bench, Coach Chuck Noll took the rookie by the ear and told him, "We're the Pittsburgh Steelers. We *live* in the end zone. The next time you go there, try to act like it's not your first time."

The Steelers of the 1970s didn't do much in the way of post-play exhibitions, and the Dallas Cowboys of that era behaved the same way. I can't prove it, but I suspect Coach Tom Landry lectured his team, "When you score a touchdown, just drop the ball in the end zone or hand it to an official on your way to the sideline. Act like it's no big deal. Don't waste any of your energy after the play is over and never, ever do anything to stir up the opposition; they're tough enough to beat without you giving them extra incentive."

But many players these days spurn that philosophy. I think they're selfish players, not team-oriented at all. They do all they can to attract attention to themselves and belittle the opposition. Defensive players, especially, like to get in an opponent's face and talk trash, trying to intimidate him. That's not allowed at lower levels of competition and I wish it was strictly banned at the professional level, too.

A friend of mine was a high school football official. He told me of officiating a one-sided game when, late in the fourth quarter, a running back for the losing team broke into the open and was on his way to a sure touchdown. As he neared the goal line, he held the ball back toward a pursuing defender. The officials immediately whistled the play dead at that spot and imposed a 15-yard unsportsmanlike penalty.

The losing team didn't score and lost the game in a shutout.

Poetic justice in my mind. Wonder if the taunting player learned anything. Many pro players could use lessons like that.

Alas, the days of true sportsmanship seem to be fading. If you're a participant, prove me wrong. If you're a specta-tor, do everything possible to discourage boorish behavior. Let's take back our sports!

ON DRIVING

My wife and I lived and worked in the Atlanta area for over 25 years. By the time we retired and moved away, traffic had grown exponentially. Despite the freeways now having two or three times as many lanes, gridlock is common. But when traffic isn't at a standstill, the highways and byways resemble Atlanta International Raceway. People ignore speed limits, slalom from lane to lane without looking, and sometimes do so with a cell phone or cup of coffee in one hand.

Speeding

Atlanta is no different from most big cities. Many motorists in large metropolises believe speeding is a birthright. Let me stress that I like many things about Atlanta but driving in the metro area is not one of them.

I think speeding is an illusion as far as saving time is concerned. If a driver has a 10-mile commute and drives 60 mph, it'll take about 10 minutes to complete his trip. If he drives 70 mph, he can save about a minute. Only a minute! Yes, a minute is a valuable piece of time, but what will the commuter do with that extra minute? Is it going to make a major difference in his day, and at what risk? Couldn't he have begun his journey a minute earlier and reduced the risk of an accident?

Speeding provides a negligible advantage, while risking a traffic citation (a ticket stop alone will take way more than a minute, not to mention beaucoup bucks). The DOT has engineers who determine the safe speed on each stretch of roadway. To drive faster is to put yourself and other motorists at risk of injury or even death.

Speeders must be supremely confident in their superior driving ability. Maybe that confidence is well-placed, but what about their fellow motorists?

The faster the vehicle is moving, the greater the damage in the event of an accident. The other guy may be inattentive, on the phone, or (heaven forbid) texting. You may be a truly superior driver, but if the other guy is distracted or impaired, your driving skills won't matter much. As illustrated above, speeding saves only a minute or so, hardly worth the risk.

Soon after the oil embargo in the early '70s, Congress declared a 55-mph maximum speed throughout the country. Traffic deaths for the next 12 months were reduced by 5000. Speed kills.

Here's a little quiz that may be informative: First, suppose a vehicle collides with a parked locomotive. At what speed would the vehicle need to be traveling before death is probable? Second, suppose a vehicle collides head-on with an identical vehicle traveling at the identical speed. At what speed to you presume death would be probable?

Have you got answers to those two questions in your mind?

I don't know the correct answers, but here's the point: Most folks would have a larger number for their answer to the first question, where a vehicle collides with an immovable object. But the answer to both questions should be the same.

Are you scratching your head over that last statement?

Let me explain: If a vehicle plows into a similar vehicle that's standing still, the parked vehicle will be driven backwards and much of the shock diminished. But if the other vehicle is traveling the same speed as the first vehicle, both vehicles come to an immediate halt, just as if the first vehicle had hit a parked locomotive.

Lesson to be Learned: The chance of death can occur at a much lower speed than most folks would presume.

Pedestrians are People, Too
Many motorists are territorial, barely tolerating other motorists and totally disdaining pedestrians. Most states have a law to the effect, "A motorist shall yield the right-of-way to a pedestrian, even if the pedestrian is in the wrong."

There are good reasons for such laws. First, a pedestrian should not be made to pay with his life for a momentary lapse. Second, there are motorists out there who would say, "Yes officer, I saw the pedestrian, but I knew I had the right-of-way, so I ran over him to teach him a lesson."

If you're a pedestrian, do all you can to ingratiate yourself to motorists. Yield the right-of-way even when it belongs to you. Move to the far side of the road or off the roadway completely when a vehicle approaches. Wave and smile; you probably won't make many friends this way, but you just might convince some motorists that you, too, are a flesh-and-blood human being and not just an annoying traffic obstacle.

To allow for an inattentive motorist, walk or run on the left side of the road, facing oncoming traffic. If you have any kind of a problem with a motorist, it'll be with the one in your lane. If you are in the right lane, the likely problem will come from behind and you'll never know what hit you. But if you're in the left lane, you'll see the problem and have plenty of time to react.

Again, conflicts between motorists and pedestrians seem to be more common in larger communities. I'm a runner and that's where I had most of my problems. I recall running a regular route and having motorists change lanes to force me onto the shoulder or into the ditch. While running in the dark and well off to the side, I had motorists turn on their bright lights. I'm sure they weren't trying to light up the night for me; rather, they were sending me a message to get off their road and don't come back.

Whether you're a pedestrian or a motorist, be polite, courteous, and friendly to all others on the roadway. We're all in this together.

Right-of-Way

Some folks in bigger cities tend to be rude drivers. I think there are several reasons for that. First, traffic is much heavier, and drivers believe they must be aggressive if they are to get out onto a busy street; he who hesitates is lost, they think. Second, with a huge population, they think they're anonymous, so their rudeness will be, too.

I've often wondered how many times a rude driver arrives at work only to have his boss or fellow worker say, "Why'd you cut me off down the street? You almost killed me!"

I'd feel so good if I knew that happened often.

Maybe you, too, have noticed how many people arrive at a red light and pull ahead of the white line in their lane. Even if they see the red light a block away, they somehow wind up ahead of the white line, possibly obstructing a left turn from a side street. I recall trying to make a left turn, but the driver to my left was two car-lengths into the intersection. I gave him a dirty look, thinking that would chastise and shame him, but he just looked at me and laughed.

Is there an epidemic of poor depth perception in this country?

The same person who pulls ahead of the white line is probably the same person who'd give you a dirty look if you were anywhere near the white line when he was making a left turn; in other words, he'd want to drive in your lane as he turned the corner.

And then there's the guy who swings out to the left when making a right turn. That's something you might need to do if you're pulling a load of hay or driving an 18-wheeler, but not with a regular-size vehicle. Either those folks have too much vehicle or too little skill. That makes anyone in the other lane fair game for a fender-bender.

Me First

I'd love to have a nickel for every time I've had a driver on a side street *accelerate* through a stop sign to pull out in front of me, often when there's no one behind me. If that driver had come to a normal stop, I'd have been through the intersection before he could take his foot off the brake. But somehow getting in front of me was critical. (Maybe he's so used to merging into heavy traffic that he barges out from of force of habit.) Then an astonishing thing happens: I slam on my brakes of course, and then creep along for six blocks while the other driver slowly accelerates up to 35 mph. He couldn't wait to get out in front of me, but once that's accomplished he has all the time in the world! Just had to show me who's boss, I guess.

And then there's the driver who passes me and, even before getting all the way back in my lane, flips on his left turn signal and hits the brakes. He saves himself one or two seconds by passing me. Meanwhile, I had to stand on the brakes to avoid a rear-end collision and then wait for him to turn, possibly costing me a minute or more in commuting time. Apparently, his time is infinitely more valuable than mine. Wonder how he'd feel if our roles were reversed. I think we know.

It's times like those I wish my vehicle was equipped with a grill-mounted .50-caliber machinegun.

In a perfect world, motorists would never do anything to force another motorist on the main thoroughfare to touch the brake or even take his foot off the gas. A motorist on a main thoroughfare should do his best to maintain a constant speed and other motorists should help him do that.

My bride and I now live in a smaller town, where driving habits are much more civil. Oh, there's the occasional rude driver, but their vehicle usually bears an out-of-state plate—if not, I presume they're transplants from a larger city. I had lunch with an Atlanta friend one day and told him about the laid-back drivers we have in our area. "We have squabbles at four-way stops, too," I said, "but instead of running over each other to get through the intersection first, we have arguments, saying, 'You go first.' 'No, you go first!'"

Whenever there's road construction in our area, traffic moves smoothly and quickly, as compared to many other areas. For example, when there's a sign announcing, "Right Lane Closed in 2000 Feet," everyone immediately gets into the left lane and we get through the construction zone at nearly the speed limit. In some areas of the country, such a sign is a signal for many drivers to switch to the right lane and accelerate, trying to get to the front of the line. Once there, they'll force their way back into the left lane. At that point, the construction zone becomes a true bottleneck with traffic flow at a near standstill. Those drivers just don't seem to understand they are the problem.

I much prefer the laid-back traffic where I now live. Too bad everyone can't see the wisdom of polite driving habits.

ON POLITICS

I'm going to do my level best not to reveal my political leanings—I don't want you skipping to the next chapter or throwing this book against the wall in disgust. Those folks who do not think exactly as I do are completely wrongheaded, of course, but there are a lot of them and I want them to read this book, too.

Political Politesse

I send occasional flaming arrows (Letters to the Editor) to the local paper. In them, I state my views as succinctly as possible. However, I try to do so diplomatically so as not to offend anyone.

As sensitively as I try to convey my thoughts, not everyone accepts them in the spirit intended. I once had a lady chastise me severely over my stated opinions. "You have to realize," she said, "that your opinions are very hurtful to those of us on the other side. You should try to temper your thoughts so as not to hurt our feelings."

Gee, I thought that was exactly what I had done.

I didn't want our talk to get out of hand, or I could have challenged her to rewrite one of my opinions so that it would be soothing to her but without diluting any of the key points. Bet she couldn't have done it.

Some folks have trouble entertaining opposing views, but I like to see what the other side is thinking. Apparently, some folks have no interest whatever in what the other side is thinking. I've got a close friend who frequently declares, "I could never vote for anyone in your party, not under any circumstances."

Does he sound like an informed voter? He doesn't to me.

We get along just fine. When we're together for very long, our conversation will get around, at least peripherally, to current events. Oddly, he and I can discuss all the hot-button topics of the day and never step on one another's toes. I can declare my opinions without ruffling a feather, so long as I don't mention either a specific politician or political party; if I did, he'd probably dig in his heels. He seems to follow the same guidelines, or else he's just nodding his head and uttering platitudes to placate me.

We can discuss nearly anything and seem to agree wholeheartedly. That makes me wonder how he can vote the way he does, but I don't think I'll bring that paradox to his attention. Gee, could he be thinking the same thing about me?

The important thing is we discuss without cussing.

Discussing politics in any forum should be as polite as possible. You'll win few converts with harsh words but may lose some friends. While I don't understand my friend's line of reasoning, pointing that out could hurt his feelings.

The Constitution

When you ask someone why the Puritans came to this country, you'll probably get words including *religious freedom*. That's true of course—that is one of the motivations for the folks who came here on the Mayflower—but there's another related reason: To get a fair shake in the court system.

England did not have a set of guiding documents like our Constitution and Bill of Rights. Thus, a judge's rulings were based solely on his (don't think they had any lady judges in those days) opinions and biases. If the judge was anti-Puritan, which many of them were, the results were predictable.

While they may not realize it, folks today who declare our Constitution a living document are harking back to the bad, old days of Victorian England when the law was whatever the judge said it was. Folks who trumpet our Constitution as a living document do so only when they can't get their way through normal means, but if they did get their way and a judge's interpretation of the Constitution became arbitrary, they'd be very disappointed with many future rulings.

If our Constitution needs updating, there's a process to do that. It's called a constitutional amendment and it has plenty of safeguards to prevent unwise, arbitrary, or mob-rule revisions. By mob-rule I mean a simple majority vote. Rather, a constitutional amendment requires at least a two-thirds vote in both the Senate and House of Representatives to pass.

Our forefathers were prescient in organizing this country at its inception. They foresaw the pitfalls of majority rule and designed instruments to prevent it.

Democracy or Republic
Even Franklin Delano Roosevelt sometimes referred to our system of government as a democracy, but it isn't. It's a representative republic and there's a major difference. A democracy is ruled by the majority; everyone votes on everything. A simple 51 percent (actually just one more than half)

of the people can impose their will on the rest. In a case like slavery, we might never have gotten rid of it had we been a true democracy.

Democracies never last too long. Gradually, citizens realize they can vote themselves largesse from the public coffers, such as: Everyone gets a million dollars on his birthday. Shortsighted folks might think that was a good idea, and if the majority was shortsighted it'd be the law of the land. It wouldn't start out that drastically, but a democracy soon devolves to that level and the country would quickly be out of business. Democracy has been tried often and it never works for very long.

A representative republic, on the other hand, must have a Constitution. Representatives and Senators elected by the citizens represent them in Congress where they create and pass laws. Those laws are restricted by the Constitution and the veto power of the President, thus avoiding the pitfalls of democracy. A rogue Congress could pass a bad law, but the veto power of the President is designed to prevent it. Likewise, a 2/3 majority in each chamber of Congress can override a presidential veto. That's also part of our system of checks and balances.

Electoral College

We've had several national elections wherein the victor didn't get the most votes. "Foul!" some cried. "The will of the people has been suppressed."

The Electoral College is another of the safeguards our forefathers installed in our system of government. Otherwise, as our population is currently distributed the east and west coasts would elect our President every four years, because that's where a majority of our population lives. Coastal residents certainly should have a say in general elections, and they do but they shouldn't have *all* the say. Remember that we are a representative republic, not a democracy. If elections were won by majority vote, we'd be a long way toward a democracy and that wouldn't be good.

Wyoming has two US senators, just like California and other more-populous states. That makes Wyoming over-represented in the US Senate. However, Wyoming has only one representative, making it under-represented in the House of Representatives. For every plus in our government, there's a minus.

See how it all balances out? Our founding fathers were geniuses!

In the founding days of our country, someone asked Benjamin Franklin what sort of government they'd be getting. He replied, "A representative republic, if you can keep it."

Depending on what just happened to their favored party, people are liable to demand democratic elections. A republican form of government isn't perfect, but it's better than anything else that's available. Republic good, democracy bad—don't ever forget that.

ON ABORTION

I thought about putting abortion in the chapter on politics. I maintain there are few subjects as politicized as abortion (can you recall a national election where the subject wasn't front and center?), but it's such a vast subject that it deserves a chapter all by itself. This book doesn't have a chapter On Crime, or that's where I'd put my thoughts on abortion!

Does that clarify my position on the subject?

We're talking murder here, the taking of a human life while still in the womb, and here's my reasoning.

DNA

Analysis of deoxyribonucleic acid is one of the most accurate forensic tools in the law enforcement arsenal. Everyone in the world has a unique DNA, and human DNA is distinctly different from that of any other living thing. DNA analysis often results in a criminal conviction when no other evidence is available. Since no two humans have identical DNA, if authorities can get a DNA match from a crime scene and a suspect, case solved!

So, if a piece of tissue (bone, muscle, etc.) has human DNA, it must be human. When does DNA originate?

During conception, a sperm cell penetrates the egg and—*voila!*—DNA is produced. Therefore, a human being is created at conception. Destroying a fetus at any point after conception is the destruction of a human being.

Allow me to go biblical for a minute just in case that helps to bring you around to my way of thinking. From Jeremiah 1:5, the Lord said, "Before I formed you in the womb I knew you." I'm guessing that's the passage the Pope was reading way back when he declared contraception verboten for Catholics. I'm also supposing that protestants and some other religions rationalized a different interpretation by saying, *Since contraception is being used, there can be no conception and therefore no subversion of God's will.* But here we're talking about contraception before the fact, not abortion, which is an extreme, after-the-fact means of contraception.

Somehow, in 1973 the Supreme Court of the United States decided our Constitution and Bill of Rights guarantee a woman's right to an abortion. In Roe v Wade, Justice Harry Blackmun wrote the opinion for the 7-2 majority. The Constitution is neither a large nor complicated document, and I defy you or anyone else to find the part that even hints at, let alone guarantees, a right to an abortion. This is one of those cases of judicial activism, an arbitrary ruling unsupported by any applicable documents. That's just what our forefathers feared and is an example of what the Puritans fled.

Our system of checks and balances is supposed to include the Supreme Court of the United States. The SCOTUS often overrules the President and Congress, but I don't recall an example of the reverse. We all probably can recall cases where that should have happened. For me, it's Roe v. Wade.

Jane Roe, the person who instigated the court case a few years before it came before the SCOTUS, was a lady named Norma McCorvey. (Incidentally, she later changed her stripes and became an ardent pro-lifer. She passed away in 2017.) In the early 1970s her life was anything but stable. Unmarried, she had a baby on the way and wanted to abort it. She lived in Texas where laws allowed an abortion only to save the life of the mother. That's why McCorvey went to court. As we know, she won her case, but not until a few years after her baby had been born and given up for adoption.

The heart of McCorvey's argument was that her right to privacy was guaranteed by the 1st, 4th, 5th, 9th, and 14th Amendments to the Constitution. So, she argued it's okay to kill a human being if you do it privately.

Isn't that exactly what she was saying?

And the Supreme Court agreed with her!

A good friend and very smart man pointed out that tubal pregnancies endanger the life of the mother. As I've stated, I have no problem with an abortion to save a mother's life but that's not what's happening in most cases. Abortions are being performed primarily as a means of post-coital birth control. The mother either had careless intercourse or later changed her mind about having a baby. In some cases, the couple may have taken adequate precautions that just didn't work, but that's not a reason to kill a fetus.

Pro-Choice advocates (more accurately, Pro-Death advocates) declare that a woman has a right to do whatever she chooses with her own body. I can't quibble with that, except I don't think she has a right to kill an unborn baby who just happens to be residing in her womb.

Adoption

Pro-Choice advocates also declare that abortion should be allowed to protect the mental health of the mother.

It seems to me that a woman's mental health would be at greater risk knowing she'd had her fetus killed. Bearing and raising a child can be a trying experience but should be far less risky to a mother's mental health than murder. If a woman just doesn't want to raise a being she helped to conceive, she should opt for adoption. With adoption, there'd be no child to raise and no fetus murdered. The mother's mental health should be as safe as possible. There are plenty of barren couples out there who would love to give a newborn a great home and upbringing. It's true that not all newborns would be adopted; some would need to be raised in orphanages but that's way better than being murdered.

Oddly, many of the same folks who advocate abortion on demand, declaring a fetus nothing but a bunch of meaningless cells, also rationalize *double* homicide in the case of a fetus who dies when its mother is murdered. Does anyone else see a dichotomy there?

As stated, Texas law in the 1970s allowed abortion to prevent the death of the mother. I agree with that position. My mind is not so made up in the case of rape or incest; maybe if there's an accompanying police report to that effect.

Pro-Choice advocates argue that restricting abortion in any way would force women to seek back-alley abortions, a very dangerous and unsanitary procedure often performed by unqualified personnel. Making the abortion less accessible would make women much more careful, realizing there could be serious consequences to promiscuity or careless conjugal sex.

Going for a Record

In the year 2014, about a fifth of all pregnancies were aborted in the US, a total over 650 thousand. We hit the disgraceful peak in 1990 with nearly one-and-a-half million abortions. There've been 58 million abortions in this country since the Roe v Wade decision.

Once abortion became legal, many organizations were formed or reorganized to accommodate this new women's right. Among them was Planned Parenthood, formed by Margaret Sanger, an avowed racist who advocated abortion as a means of controlling the growth of the black population.

She's been very successful, with abortions in the black community accounting for 40 percent of the total in this country.

Bear in mind that blacks make up only an eighth of our population.

Here are a few of Sanger's quotes (gag reflex alert):

- *The most merciful thing that a family does to one of its infant members is to kill it.*
- *A free race cannot be born of slave mothers.*
- *When motherhood becomes the fruit of a deep yearning, not the result of ignorance or accident, its children will become the foundation of a new race.*
- *A woman's physical satisfaction was more important than any marriage vow.*

If you have the stomach for even more such quotes, do an internet search on "Margaret Sanger, in her own words."

Abortion became legal on the heels of the sexual revolution of the late 1960s, and that aggravated the situation. Free love advocates then could mate like rabbits and, if worse came to worst, just get an abortion. No big deal! We ought to have more respect for ourselves, for our bodies, and for unborn human beings. Killing fetuses should never be a casual thing.

Incidentally, as I write this, Congress has just seen fit to continue funding Planned Parenthood. Put another way, they're subsidizing murder.

ON INTELLECTUALS

Many of our politicians are exceptionally bright. In fact, most of them probably are way above average. If they also have common sense and practical experience, we're in great shape but that doesn't always happen.

Starting at the Top

I have a stepson who was a whiz in college, graduating *summa cum laude* from a good college. *Summa cum laude* is the upper echelon of the best of all college graduates, the best of the best. He had many job interviews upon graduation, but not one offer to become chief executive officer, chairman of the board, or any such management position. Potential employers probably thought he was book smart but not street smart; they were looking for someone with practical experience. Instead, he had to settle for a worker-bee job. After moving around to a few other similar positions to broaden his experience, he finally landed an executive position. He's in upper management now, but likely would have been a disaster had he started his career there.

Some of our politicians got out of college and went straight to the State House or Washington. They've never run so much as a lemonade stand, yet they're in position to affect people and businesses all over the state or country. They've never been in the real world, yet they *know* how it should work.

That last statement could be said of many entertainers and professors, too. Hollywood and academia are Ivory Towers. Entertainers have plenty of face time in the media and their pompous discourse is mostly harmless, just annoying. Professors mold the minds of students in their classes, yet few of them have even a partial grasp on how things work outside their campuses. Many students come out of college thinking just like their professors—why not, they've never been in the real world either. I maintain that college graduates should live in the real world for a while before they enter government and tell the rest of us how things should work.

Voters need to determine how well a candidate did in positions of responsibility. If previous performance is marginal or worse, choose another candidate. If there is no previous performance to judge, you might want to vote for someone else. At least five years of practical experience would be good, 10 would be better, before being elected to make decisions that affect us all.

Nothing but the Best
We need smart people, very smart people, at all levels of government, but they need to have their feet on the ground. Theory, good intentions, and wishful thinking doesn't cut it. We should be very selective about who we put in positions of power. Pay little heed to a candidate's recent job descriptions; instead focus on results in those positions. Because a candidate has held high-level positions means little; results are what counts. I'll bet you can think of at least one

candidate who held a very prestigious position, but was a practical disaster in that job. If a candidate has produced good results in the past, likely he'll produce good results in the future.

We've had our share of idiot savants in office, folks who were book-smart but had no common sense or idea of how things work where the rubber meets the road. We've survived such incompetence so far, but that doesn't mean we always will.

ON GUN CONTROL

As I write this, a school shooting is just hitting the news. I know when I read the morning paper there'll be a barrage of demands for more gun control. We're going to spend a few minutes analyzing that strategy from all angles.

The Illusion of Action

Politicians are among those calling for more gun control, but not because they have practical ideas on how to stop gun violence. They just want to give constituents the illusion of being proactive by proposing feel-good laws that won't have any real effect on the problem. By the way, many of those politicians have armed bodyguards who wouldn't be affected by the proposed laws. Apparently, it's good for the lords to be protected and safe, but not the peasants.

Allowing that some politicians propose new gun laws with the best of intentions, we need to insist that those proposed laws would have a beneficial effect. Many politicians and their constituents are content with good intentions; they ignore the results, even if the results produce an undesired effect. You'll see that on many political fronts, not just gun control.

It's already illegal to have a firearm on school property in most cases. The perpetrators know that. Do you suppose a would-be school shooter ever saw the sign "No Guns on School Property," then turned around and left the premises? Of course not. He probably read the sign this way: "The Shooting Gallery is Open." That's exactly why shooters choose places like schools, movie theaters, and malls where no one is supposed to be armed. Gun free zones are in fact free-fire zones.

Have you ever noticed there's never a mass shooting at a gun store or gun show? Did you ever wonder why?

In the case of school shootings, I can think of a more effective deterrent: Post signs at all entrances to the effect, "Only Staff and Faculty May Possess Firearms on School Property." To go a bit further, make it known that all staff and faculty have taken mandatory firearms and concealed carry training. It wouldn't be necessary to require such people to carry firearms, just the knowledge that they *might* be able to shoot back would be a powerful deterrent to would-be killers.

All teachers should be trained on firearms use, even the ones who just aren't comfortable with guns. A coach at the Parkland, Florida, school shooting used himself as a human shield to protect students. He died in his efforts. Suppose that hero had been allowed to carry a firearm. He not only might still be alive, he might have taken out the shooter and saved other lives. Or maybe the shooter would have killed him anyway. If so, one of the other staff members, even one with an aversion to firearms, might have had an epiphany and been moved to pick up the coach's gun, and then gone down the hall to neutralize the shooter blazing away at a roomful of defenseless students.

Even anti-gun teachers probably would prefer to shoot the shooter, rather than see dozens of students killed.

Teachers should not be required to carry a concealed weapon, but some would be happy to do so, especially if it involved a bump up in pay. Among those are ex-military and ex-law enforcement personnel. Other teachers without such credentials might still be proficient in firearms use and willing to help defend their school.

A teachers' primary responsibility is teaching, but when a shooter is on campus that responsibility broadens. There won't be any teaching when there's a shooter roaming the school's hallways. Folks like the Parkland coach would be moved to act, but empty hands won't do the trick.

Some schools have School Resource Officers who are armed and present for the sole purpose of maintaining law and order. That's great, if a school can afford an SRO. Some schools are so large that several SROs would be needed to be effective. If a school can't afford that considerable expense, they should consider allowing teachers to carry concealed firearms. That might warrant a slight bonus for this extra duty, but quite a few teachers could be armed for less money than the salary of an SRO and be less obvious to anyone contemplating mayhem.

But our current solution to school shootings is to disarm even more potential victims. Really?

The President and First Family are protected by armed Secret Service personnel. Politicians and celebrities are protected by armed bodyguards. Even football coaches are escorted by armed guards as they cross the field to shake hands with their counterparts.

Meanwhile, our school children are protected by…nothing! Yet some of the most vociferous voices on the subject claim we don't need anyone with a gun to protect them.

How's that working so far?

If armed personnel are a good way to protect presidents, politicians, entertainers, and coaches, why wouldn't it be a good way to protect students?

There are some assassins who have a death wish. There are plenty of examples where someone killed many people before using the last bullet on himself. Had any of the victims been armed, they might have sent the perpetrator to his eternal reward before he did too much damage.

Is there a chance a good guy could hit an innocent victim with defensive fire?

That depends on the proficiency of the shooter, and that's why proper training is a must. But it's for certain the perpetrator would go on killing otherwise. An armed and well-trained teacher, SRO, or custodian could minimize the damage in most of these incidents.

Along with armed staff and faculty, metal detectors at all school entrances would be another positive measure, although tending it might be labor intensive, considering how many legitimate items might trigger the alarm and require someone to check them out. Limiting access to schools could also help deter would-be killers. Each school in Israel, for example, has only one entrance, and it's manned by an armed guard. No reason we couldn't learn from someone else's success.

Zero Guns

The most ardent gun control folks advocate completely ridding our country of guns. They often decry the existence of 300 million guns in this country, as though that pinpoints a problem. The number of guns in this country has increased, admittedly, but no more than the rate of population growth. The ratio of guns to people is about the same, but the number of school shootings has risen dramatically. School shootings were almost unheard of 30 or 40 years ago. That should tell us that guns are not the problem—it's the people!

There are plenty of theories on why that is, such as violent movies and video games, but they're just theories so we won't spend time on them here.

Every time there's a mass shooting, some politicians cry for a total gun ban. They're seizing on a crisis to try to implement their unrelated agenda: They know they'll never eliminate guns completely, but they'd love to disarm the law-abiding public.

I've done my best to avoid clichés, but I'm going to use one here: "Armed people are citizens; disarmed people are subjects." The first thing dictators like Hitler and Stalin did was disarm as many people as possible, making it hard for them to resist tyranny.

"Oh, but that would never happen here," anti-gun proponents would argue. "We would never do anything to take advantage of an unarmed public."

Assuming they're sincere, what about future administrations? Can today's anti-gunners guarantee that those in power 10 or 20 years from now will have the same benevolent attitude?

Zero Guns Equals *More* Crime

Trying to eliminate guns completely would be a disaster, just like Prohibition didn't purge our country of alcoholic beverages. Making all guns illegal would create a new windfall for organized crime. They'd either set up clandestine weapons manufacturing facilities or smuggle firearms into this country, probably both.

Completely eliminating firearms is a dream that will never happen, and it's not even a noble objective. How would the proverbial little old lady defend herself against crack addicts who broke into her apartment in the dead of night?

If neither the little old lady nor the thugs had a firearm, guess how that would turn out. But, if the little old lady had a firearm and knew how to use it, the odds could swing in her favor. We've all seen the Colt Single-Action Army revolver, the one Matt Dillon and every other western movie character carried. That firearm has several monikers: First, it's called the Great Equalizer for the exact reason just stated. The second nickname is The Peacemaker. When potential victims are armed, crime goes down. Criminals much prefer easy pickings.

Suppose a dope fiend broke down your back door, intent on murdering you and then ransacking your home:

1. Would you be able to dial 9-1-1 before he did you in?
2. Would you be able to tell the desk sergeant the necessary information before you died?
3. Would the desk sergeant be able to relay that information before you expired?
4. Would the officer, coincidentally parked at the curb in front of your house, be able to respond in time to save your life?

The answer to those questions, certainly the last few, is NO!

But suppose you had a firearm in your bedside table and knew how to use it, can you foresee a better outcome?

Firearms in the wrong hands can take lives, but firearms in the right hands can save lives. There will always be firearms in the wrong hands. We need to be sure we honest citizens are not disarmed, or the results are predictable.

The local paper carried a spate of anti-gun Letters to the Editor a few years ago. I sent a response to the *Daily Planet*:

> *To the Editor: There have been quite a few anti-gun letters in this space recently. I believe even the most ardent of those authors know that guns can prevent crime. Here's challenge to them to prove my point:*
>
> *I want to place a sign in your front yard to the effect, "These premises are proudly gun-free." I will pay for the sign and its upkeep; you'll have artistic control to ensure compliance with your aesthetic sensibilities. The sign must remain in place for at least a year, be lit for easy reading from the street day or night, and it must be bilingual so our Latino friends can share your pride.*

Gee, no one took me up on my generous offer. Imagine that!

NRA and Concealed Carry

Gun control advocates hate both things. They portray the National Rifle Association as a group of bloodthirsty gunslingers who'd shoot first and ask questions later. They feel the same about citizens with concealed carry permits.

The facts are that neither of these groups is a threat to civilized society. Crime rates for both groups are a tiny fraction of one percent, almost negligible. NRA members are law-abiding citizens interested in defending their own property and lives, and that of others. Concealed carry permit holders have gone through extensive background checks;

their criminal and health records (mental and physical) have been carefully evaluated; if the applicant doesn't pass all checks with flying colors, no permit is issued.

Once a person has been granted permission to carry a concealed firearm, the permit should be honored throughout the country. Some states do have reciprocal agreements, but that courtesy needs to be universal. There's no reason for a person being able to defend himself in his home state, but not in another.

Ban Certain Guns

"Ban assault rifles," gun control advocates tell us. "There's no need for an honest person to have one. Also, there's no need for high-capacity magazines in any weapon."

Forty years ago, the firearm carried by most law enforcement people was a .38 caliber, six-shot revolver. As time progressed they found themselves outgunned by criminals carrying semi-automatic pistols with high-capacity magazines; criminals could shoot faster and longer. To have much of a chance in a firefight, law enforcement, too, had to carry pistols with more than six shots available. That's also about the time the police, SWAT teams, etc. began using military-style rifles since that's what some bad guys were using.

The term assault rifle is a catchphrase for gun control advocates, evoking visions of a madman blazing away at helpless victims for a seeming eternity. Military carry assault rifles, but they're capable of fully automatic fire—the gun keeps shooting as long as there's a finger pulling the trigger. Firearms with that capability are very rare in civilian hands, and then only with a very extensive background check.

A single-shot firearm is an assault rifle if it's used to shoot someone, but advocates of firearms bans probably mean military-style rifles such as an AR-15, which doesn't have fully automatic fire capability. "Such rifles have no legitimate civilian application," they declare. "Additionally, such firearms typically have high-capacity magazines, which also have no peaceful purpose."

Aside from organized shooting matches, military-style rifles are becoming more the norm in such pastimes as varmint shooting. An afternoon of plinking at a prairie dog town, for example, can result in expending many hundreds of rounds. That's a solid argument for having a high-capacity magazine.

True, some mass murderers use military-style rifles, and so do the police who apprehend them. Until the police arrive, shouldn't potential victims be able to defend themselves adequately? When the bad guys realize their targets are equally-armed, they may seek easier prey.

Why Gun Control Won't Work
As stated, most gun control advocates are politicians who want to give the impression of trying to stop crime. The city of Chicago has some of the most restrictive gun laws in the country—gun stores are illegal there, just to give you an idea—yet the city has one of the country's highest gun homicide rates. That may be because, despite notoriously tough gun laws, Chicago has notoriously lax enforcement; punishment for illegally having or using a gun in committing a crime is often a mere slap on the wrist. In some cases, the gun charge is dropped completely in return for a guilty plea to a lesser crime.

That's a step in the wrong direction. Whether a gun is used in committing a crime or whether an unauthorized person is carrying a gun, pleading down a gun crime should never happen. Quite the opposite. If someone commits robbery with a firearm, he's threatening to kill the victim if he doesn't cooperate. Thus, it seems an armed robber should be liable for attempted murder—he'd have pulled the trigger if things hadn't gone his way.

The courts are backed up and plea deals are necessary to lighten the load, I get that. But reducing or dismissing firearms charges against would-be gunmen is not the answer.

Not to pick on Chicago, other cities with strict gun laws also have a high incidence of gun violence. Duh, gun laws only affect law-abiding citizens, not criminals. Criminals would be happy to see stricter gun laws since their victims wouldn't be able to defend themselves. Many prison surveys indicate that a criminal's greatest fear is not the police, or dogs, or alarms, it's an armed victim.

Criminals aren't going to obey gun laws no matter how comprehensive they are; that's why they're called criminals. Stricter gun laws just make it harder for honest citizens to resist crime.

Gun control advocates often claim civilians have no need for firearms to protect themselves; that's what the police are for, they say.

Not exactly. Police carry firearms to protect themselves, not civilians. Police interrupting a robbery or murder and saving the victim is a very unusual occurrence. If a civilian is unarmed, he has no defense at all. Typically, police arrive, draw a white line around the body, and question potential witnesses. The perpetrator has fled the scene and the crime itself is long over.

The first thing a criminal does before committing a crime is to be sure there are no police in the area. They like totally defenseless victims. To use another cliché, "When seconds count, the police are only minutes away."

In nearly every instance, if a victim wants to stop a crime, he'll need to do it himself.

ON THE DEATH PENALTY

On February 15, 1933, Chicago mayor Anton Cermak was shot by Giuseppe Zangara who intended to kill President Franklin Roosevelt but missed. Cermak died on March 6, and Zangara was executed two weeks later. Thirty-five years earlier, William McKinley's assassin was dispatched about seven months after the event. Justice swift and sure.

But that was then, this is now. Had the Cermak event happened today, Zangara's case likely wouldn't have gone to court for years (ditto for McKinley's murderer). With hundreds of eyewitnesses he'd still have been convicted but execution, if such was prescribed, could have been delayed for decades. Attorneys just can't amass billable hours if justice is meted out in weeks or months.

Death penalty opponents decry the practice as cruel and unusual, that it's barbaric and offers the convict no chance for repentance. And finally, opponents are in fear of executing an innocent man.

We don't draw and quarter convicts in this country; our methods of execution are at least as humane as those administered by the convict upon his victims. It's neither cruel and unusual nor barbaric. The murderer didn't allow his victim a chance to get right with God before he died, so there's no reason to go out of our way to allow the murderer that opportunity. As far as the possibility of executing an innocent man is concerned, with modern forensics (e.g., DNA testing) that possibility is near non-existent. Also, with justice swift and sure, the murder rate would drop dramatically, thereby making the chance of a false conviction near impossible.

By the way, capital punishment is never administered for crimes of passion, only for premeditated murder.

With justice tenuous and delayed, a murderer is little deterred realizing that he'll likely be breathing air for at least a decade. A man recently convicted of murdering his wife is predicted to be on death row for 25 years before he gets the needle. He may not get the needle even then. With so many appeals available, nay *mandatory* in capital punishment cases, there's a chance of a jury or judge ruling in the murderer's favor. The longer a case drags on the more a witness' memory fades, making the upholding of a previous conviction tenuous.

Here's one for the record books: In 1988, Richard Farley burst into his workplace in Sunnyvale, California, opening fire and shooting 11 people, seven of which died. He was convicted and sentenced to execution, but he's still alive— 30 years after the fact!

Justice swift and sure?

Not exactly, but delays such as this are becoming more common, not the exception, and not just in California.

We don't owe mercy to a convicted murderer, but we do owe justice to the victim's family. How can they possibly have closure knowing the murderer is breathing the same air they are, while their beloved is in the cold, cold ground?

We can debate this subject forever, but one thing that's inarguable: Following capital punishment, the rate of recidivism drops to zero!

ON TAXES

We need things like infrastructure and national defense, and the only way to pay for them is by collecting taxes. Just understand that paying taxes is a cost of doing business for everyone and is part of the overhead for companies and corporations. Any tax at all increases overhead and reduces profitability, but taxes are a necessary evil, no doubt about it.

Taxes and Federal Revenue

Taxes and federal revenue do not have a linear relationship. For example, if the tax rate went from 20 percent to 30 percent, federal revenue would not go up 50 percent; it might even go down. That's because raising the tax rate reduces the profitability of any business, or in the case of the nation it reduces the profitability of all businesses. So, the government would be getting 30 percent of a smaller Gross Domestic Product (e.g., 20 percent of 20 million dollars is $4 million; 30 percent of 10 million dollars is $3 million).

We can agree that federal revenue would be zero if the tax rate was zero. That's an easy one. But maybe we wouldn't agree immediately that federal revenue would also be zero if the tax rate was 100 percent, but it's true. Let's look at that so we'll all be on the same page.

Overhead for any business is a combination of expenses. That includes such things as employee pay and benefits, cost of materials, facility upkeep, and taxes. Whatever income is left after paying all the overhead is profit. That's what the person, company, or corporation takes home.

If the tax rate was 100 percent, all income would be diverted to paying taxes. In the case of the individual, there'd be nothing to take home, nothing to buy groceries, pay rent, etc. In the case of businesses, there'd be nothing left to pay employee wages and benefits, buy materials, or keep up buildings and grounds. Taxes would eat it all and there'd be no profit. No one would stay in business if they couldn't make any profit.

That begs the question: When would federal revenue be maximum?

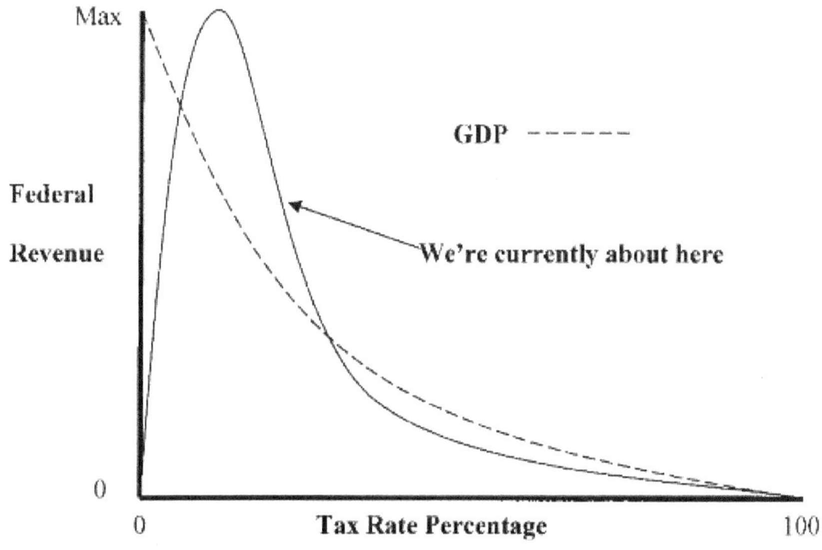

The answer is, probably with a tax rate of less than 10 percent. We've been above that for years, on average, almost since the day the government began collecting taxes. That explains why in those rare cases where there is a tax cut federal revenue goes up instead of down. If that's not perfectly clear, the accompanying diagram may help you understand.

As you can see, we're at a point where lowering tax rates will increase federal revenue. We've been in this position for many years. It happened as a result of tax cuts during the Bush II, Reagan, Kennedy, and Coolidge administrations.

Opponents of tax cuts worry about increasing the federal deficit and debt. "We'll have to reduce entitlements or something else to pay for the tax cuts," they declare.

Where were these deficit hawks when some administrations and Congress were spending like drunken sailors?

Federal revenue will go down initially when commerce diverts tax money away from Washington and toward expanding their businesses. But once those expansions kick in, federal revenue will be higher than it was before the tax cuts. The bottom line is that tax cuts pay for themselves; you just need a little patience. Based on past experience, federal revenue will go up as described within six months to a year.

Tax Cuts Benefit Only the Rich
Opponents always decry tax cuts as benefitting the rich to the detriment of everyone else. "The rich" includes the folks who employ most of us. They already pay most of the taxes in this country and their taxes would go down, but they'd use most of the tax cut to grow their businesses.

Okay, businesses would use some of their tax cuts to give their stockholders a dividend or buy themselves a new Mercedes, but most of the money would be plowed back into their businesses. At least that's what smart businessmen would do, and they wouldn't be rich in the first placc if they weren't smart.

With or without tax cuts, the case could be made that the rich don't pay any taxes, they just collect money from the rest of us and pass it on to the federal government. If you think about it, businesses will raise prices on goods and services if taxes go up, and the rest of us pay those higher prices. The only alternative businesses would have, if they couldn't raise prices, is to cut back production and lay off workers or reduce their benefits. Either way, the little guy pays.

With the big guys (employers) getting a tax cut, they can expand their businesses, hire more employees, and maybe even raise salaries and benefits. They may be forced to do the latter, because other employers would be feeling a boom, too, and competition for good workers will be high. If your boss didn't give you a raise and a bonus, someone else might.

Rich Non-Employers

Not all rich folks meet a payroll; they don't have a traditional business of their own. Most of the folks who fall into this category are investors. Their money winds up in the accounts of folks who do have regular businesses. That allows a CEO and board of directors to expand their business as if they were using the corporation's own money.

There may be some idle rich who neither run a business nor invest their money, but those folks are few and far between. Also, they may not be rich for very long.

Balance of Trade

Balance of trade is a measure of the difference between a country's imports and exports, usually exports minus imports expressed in dollars. If a country has more exports than imports, that would mean more money coming into the country than is going out. That's called a surplus and is considered a good thing because the country is turning a profit. If a country imports more than it exports, that's called a deficit and is considered bad because more money is going out than coming in; the country is losing money.

The United States is currently in a trade deficit, so how can we create a surplus balance of trade?

Some US manufacturers want our government to impose higher tariffs on incoming goods, forcing importers to charge more and thereby making domestic products more competitive, pricewise. Importers would have to raise prices on their goods to cover the cost of the higher tariff, making their prices more in line with what domestic manufacturers charge for similar goods. That would result in domestic manufacturers selling more goods in this country. However, if the US raises its tariffs, other countries are bound to raise theirs, too. The overall result might be a wash; US manufacturers would sell more domestically, but their foreign sales would go down.

A better solution might be to reduce taxes. With the resultant lower overhead, domestic manufacturers could charge less for their products, which is a better way of getting more competitive with importers. The US currently has one of the highest tax rates in the world. In other words, domestic overhead is much higher here than it is in other countries.

Some make the argument that corporate tax rates were around 90 percent back in the 1950s, and our country was booming.

That's true, but our balance of trade had an astronomical surplus. No one else in the world was manufacturing much of anything. Places like England, France, Germany, and Japan were trying to rebuild from WWII. We were the only game in town and could still make a profit despite what normally would be a crippling overhead.

Due to high corporate taxes some domestic manufacturers have moved their facilities overseas. There they can be more competitive, not only by paying lower taxes but also because labor rates are lower. We're not liable to lower labor rates in this country, but if we lower taxes enough, corporations can still pay high labor rates and be competitive with other countries.

And finally, US companies who move their operations overseas often don't bring their profits back to the States because of the punitive taxes they'd have to pay. At this writing, our government finally allowed US companies to pay a modest tax if they repatriate their foreign profits. That amount of money is estimated to be trillions of dollars. Once corporations put that money to use domestically, it should be a great boost for our economy.

State Tax Deductions

When it comes to tax time, everyone loves deductions. Me too, but I'd still like to see state tax deductions eliminated on federal returns. Here's why:

Someone who pays high state taxes can currently take a big deduction on his federal return. Meanwhile, someone in a state with low state taxes gets a much smaller deduction. So, assuming the salaries and everything else about these two people is similar, the person who pays a high state tax pays less in federal taxes. Yet that person gets the same benefits as the person who paid more in federal taxes.

People with similar incomes and other circumstances should be paying similar federal taxes. The root of the problem seems to be: Why are some state taxes so high while others are low or even non-existent?

The answer: Uninformed voters (I'm being polite here) elect politicians who are either ignorant or have a nefarious agenda.

Tax Cuts Help Everyone

When there's an across-the-board tax cut, everyone makes out. But that'd be true even if only the "evil rich" get a tax cut. Such an act wouldn't be unfair since the rich pay almost all the taxes anyway. (We've had instances where folks who pay no taxes got tax credits, a check from the government, when everyone else got a tax cut; that's beyond ridiculous! Can you say "vote buying?") With a tax cut, the business-man can expand his business and make more money. He'll hire more employees to do that, and probably raise the wages and benefits of the employees he already has.

The government likes to play Sugar Daddy and claim it's *giving* us money when we get a tax cut. But what they're really doing is letting us keep more of what was already ours. I know it means the same thing, but it affects your perspective. With a tax cut, the government isn't giving you anything, they're just *taking* less from you.

As icing on the cake, when there's a big tax cut federal revenue goes up. With the resultant expanded economy, there'll be more money going to Washington despite the lower tax rates. Lower overhead (taxes) results in higher profitability and often results in a given business paying more in taxes despite lower tax rates.

Employees might even pay more in taxes due to raises and bonuses, yet their take-home pay would still be higher than before the tax cut.

And finally, newly employed folks would be earning a

living and paying taxes instead of being a drain on the Treasury.

Everyone wins!

Well, not everyone makes out on tax cuts. There are politicians who thrive in a down economy. They claim to be champions of the poor and downtrodden, but they'd like to have even more of them. If the poor and downtrodden consider these politicians their personal source of income, they're going to vote for those politicians. Such politicians are in business strictly to get reelected and will do whatever is necessary to achieve that end.

The Fair Tax
Several years ago, Congressman John Linder and radio personality Neal Boortz published *The Fair Tax Book*. In it they espouse a flat sales tax on just about everything sold at the retail level. That sales tax would replace our current income tax and nearly every other form of taxation.

The name of the book explains it all. To wit: Wealthier people would pay the same tax rate as the less wealthy, but they'd probably pay more total taxes because they'd spend a lot more. As an example, someone who spends a million dollars a year might pay $170,000 in sales taxes, while someone who spends a $100 thousand would pay $17,000. The tax percentage paid would be the same for everyone.

The advantages of the Fair Tax are numerous. There'd be no more paying a worker under the table; when such a worker spent money at a retail establishment, he'd be paying taxes at the same rate as everyone else. There'd be no more IRS or their beaucoup forms and regulations, and no more tax preparation or audits. As a bonus, total taxes paid by most folks would be less than under the current system.

Who could be against any of that?

Additionally, everyone would have some skin in the game. We currently have quite a few people who pay little or no income tax. Some politicians preach to them that the rich aren't paying their fair share (in truth, the rich pay almost all the taxes). Many folks who pay no taxes buy that line of tripe and vote for such politicians. To ensure reelection, those politicians then try to tax the producers at ever-increasing rates. As we've explained, such actions kill our economy and are a detriment to everyone, except said politicians.

Wealthier people have lobbyists to promote their interests to Congress, and poor people have politicians who kowtow to them in exchange for votes. That leaves the middle class with not much representation; in fact, some politicians are trying to force more of them into the dependent class. Higher tax rates force employers to cut back on production and employment. That, in turn, forces more of the middle class onto Welfare rolls, just what unscrupulous politicians need to grow their constituency.

So, when can we expect the Fair Tax to be implemented?

Don't hold your breath. The Fair Tax is not favorable to many politicians, so they would never support it. Even if it were implemented somehow, the very next day (the same day?) special interest groups would begin lobbying for exemptions. Rich folks would have reasons for getting a tax rebate and poorer folks would have their reasons, too. Some politicians are in business strictly to service such special interests and they'd try to enact exemptions for their constituents. It wouldn't take long before we'd be right back where we are now, or worse.

The Fair Tax is a utopian concept, but there's probably no way to get there.

ON RELIGION

A young preacher fresh out of seminary taught my con-firmation class. He was a fire-and-brimstone kind of guy with strong opinions on all matters religious. One day he declared that only people of our faith, Lutheran, would make it to heaven. Baptists, Catholics, Methodists, and all other denominations would be out of luck.

"What about that other Lutheran congregation down the street," we asked. "Will they be up there with us?" He said they'd be toast, only folks from our specific synod would make it to heaven.

I was a young lad then, barely 13 and not the sharpest knife in the drawer, but that just didn't make sense to me. What about all those other kids in my junior high class who don't go to my church? Are they doomed to hell and eternal damnation?

Gee, they seemed like nice kids. I'd didn't want my friends to be flambéed forever.

Had the pastor put any related questions on one of his examinations, I'd have given him the answer he wanted (I wasn't dumb enough to do otherwise). But I believe folks who have faith in Christ will make it to the Promised Land, and that's the only way to get there. As an earthly bonus, folks who have faith in Christ will lead an upright, honest, God-fearing life.

Incidentally, some folks claim they don't need to go to church regularly to be a Christian. Possibly, but their faith certainly won't be getting stronger staying home on Sunday mornings, quite the opposite probably. It's kind of like riding a bicycle: you never forget how, but if you don't do it for a while…

A Little Fish in a Big Pond

One of my fascinations is astronomy. The number of stars, planets, and other heavenly bodies out there is just astronomical (perfect choice of words). Additionally, the dimensions of our universe boggle my meager mind. Whenever I begin to think I'm a person of some importance, all I do is let my mind wander to the subject of astronomy and it brings me back down to Earth. On the off chance that you've never thought too much about it, I'll attempt to bring some perspective to the subject.

First, planet Earth is about eight thousand miles in diameter and about 25 thousand miles around. (We'll start out very basic here.) That seems big and it is, at least compared to little old me. The Sun is a star and is much bigger, nearly a million miles in diameter and three million in circumference. The distance from the Earth to our Sun is about 93 million miles. It's so far away that it takes light emitted by the Sun about eight minutes to get to us. If the Sun blew a fuse, we wouldn't know about it until it got dark on Earth eight minutes later.

By the way, light travels at 186 thousand miles per second.

The Sun being so much larger than the Earth, you never see a scale model of the two. If you drew the Sun one inch in diameter, the Earth would have to be less than a hundredth of an inch (if you could even make a mark that small, could anyone see it?). That diagram might not be too practical to draw or to observe. So maybe you could make the Sun 10 inches and the Earth 1/10th of an inch. The Earth would be a little tough to see even then. It could be done, except to keep everything to scale you'd want to separate the two orbs appropriately. With a 10-inch Sun and a 1/10th inch Earth, you'd have to space the two about 80 feet apart, so you'd have to use *really big* paper.

Our Solar System (not to scale)

The Earth is in orbit around the Sun and takes an "Earth year" to make one round trip. There are seven other planets orbiting our Sun. The Sun, the planets and their moons, along with some asteroids, comets, and other space objects make up our solar system.

Mercury and Venus are closer to the Sun and orbit much faster than Earth—they must go faster to avoid falling into the Sun. All the other planets are farther away, travel much slower, have a much longer path around the sun, and take much more than an Earth year to complete an orbit.

Pluto is no longer considered a planet and is mighty indignant about that snub. Now considered a dwarf planet, Pluto was discovered 85 years ago and hasn't completed one trip around the Sun since then, a Pluto year being 248 Earth years. Pluto is about 3.5 billion miles away from the Sun, on average. I say, on average because Pluto's orbit is elliptical and not a perfect circle, as are most planetary orbits, including our own.

Gosh, we're starting to discuss some BIG numbers! Hang on, because it's going to get even more interesting.

In December 2015, astronomers found the farthest known object in our solar system. They named it V774104 (hey, they had to call it *something*). The estimated diameter is 300-600 miles and it's more than 100 times farther from the Sun than the Earth, or about nine billion miles. That makes the diameter of our solar system at least 18 billion miles.

A galaxy is a cluster of solar systems and our galaxy is called the Milky Way. Compared to other solar systems, ours is about average in size. Astronomers estimate there are 100 billion solar systems in the Milky Way. Wow! One hundred billion stars, one for each solar system (or sometimes two binary stars per solar system instead of one), plus all the other objects make for a ton of stuff floating around out there. As mentioned, our solar system is about 18 billion miles in diameter, so if the other 100 billion solar systems are about that size we must be talking about some serious distance when we discuss the size of the Milky Way.

The Milky Way is pinwheel-shaped, estimated to be 100 thousand light-years across and 10 thousand light-years thick. As mentioned earlier, light travels at 186 thousand miles per second.

If it takes light 100 thousand years to travel across the Milky Way, how far would that be?

"A fur piece," they'd say here in the South.

I'm sure you could figure it out, but I'll save you the trouble. At 186 thousand miles per second, light travels about six trillion miles in a year, a trillion being a million times a million. Therefore, the diameter of the Milky Way would be six trillion times 100 thousand, or about 600 thousand-trillion miles. Putting the mileage another way, the diameter of the Milky Way in miles is a six followed by 17 zeros.

The thickness of the Milky Way is $1/10^{th}$ of those numbers.

Since it takes light 100 thousand years to travel across the entire Milky Way, some of the light we're getting from distant stars has been *en route* for a very long time. In fact, we're still getting light from stars in our own galaxy that burned out many centuries ago. They're dead, long gone, but some of the light they emitted before dying still hasn't reached planet Earth.

Solar systems like ours are held together by gravity. The Sun, being the most massive thing in our solar system, has the most gravity and everything else is held in orbit around it. Millenniums ago, the theory goes, many celestial objects were moving in relatively straight lines when they came under the Sun's gravitational influence. Rather than continuing their paths, some objects altered course, bent around the Sun, and into orbit. Other objects came under the Sun's influence, too, but were either too far away or going too fast to be captured. They just changed direction slightly and kept going. Some unfortunate objects traveling too slowly or too close to the Sun were swallowed up and are gone forever. Guess the Earth lucked out!

Our moon is held in orbit by the gravity of the Earth, and the same is true for other planets holding their satellites.

Of the other solar systems in our galaxy, the closest to ours (Alpha Centauri) is over four light-years away.

The next question must be: What holds our galaxy together?

The answer is a black hole, a celestial object with such a strong gravitational pull that even light is drawn to it. You can't see a black hole, no matter how powerful your telescope, because its gravity is so strong that it doesn't allow light to escape. A black hole doesn't emit light, but astronomers have other ways of detecting its existence. Some light from other sources coming our direction that pass near the black hole would be sucked in and never get to us; light beams traveling past a black hole but far enough away not to be captured would have their trajectory altered, and that's how scientists can detect the existence of these monsters. Astronomers estimate the black hole at the center of the Milky Way to be less than 15 miles in diameter yet has a mass 4.5 *million* times greater than our Sun. Okay, 15 miles isn't monstrous in size, but the gravitational force of a black hole definitely is.

The Milky Way is huge yet is a very small part of the Universe, a miniscule part really. There are an estimated 100 billion other galaxies out there. The distance from the Milky Way to the next closest galaxy is an estimated one million light-years.

Our solar system is located out on one of the arms of the Milky Way's pinwheel. All the stars we can see with the naked eye, even with all but the most powerful telescopes, are located within our own galaxy.

Picture of the Milky Way, showing the Black hole in the middle (I used a special camera)

The entire Universe is estimated to be about 91 billion light-years across. To calculate how many miles that is, multiply the speed of light (six trillion miles per year) by 91 billion, which comes to the number 5.5 followed by 23 zeros. If you're planning to make that trip, be sure to pack a lunch.

As you can see, exploring our own solar system would be a project of many lifetimes; exploring the Milky Way would take billions of times longer; and to explore the Universe billions of times longer than to explore our galaxy. I'd like to stick around to try it.

As mentioned above, a galaxy is held together by the tremendous gravity of a black hole. So, what do you suppose holds a universe together?

Astronomers are reluctant to make a prediction, but your humble scribe is not inhibited at all: I think it's all held together with Gorilla Glue.

Just kidding.

In his tremendous book, *A Short History of Nearly Everything*, Bill Bryson poses the following question: "If someone went to the very edge of the Universe and peeked through the curtain, what would he see?"

He doesn't offer an answer, but I will. I think there are more universes out there, billions of them probably. So, what does it all mean?

Scientists have labored and studied for years, trying to understand the makeup of an atom. Suppose each atom was really a miniature solar system. Then the bits inside that atom could be a miniature sun (nucleus) surrounded by its own orbiting planets (electrons). A group of atoms makes up a molecule, but maybe a molecule is really a miniature galaxy. Could a collection of molecules be a universe that's really a plant, your dog, the pencil you're holding, or—you?

Going in the other direction, maybe our solar system is really a big atom, the Milky Way a giant molecule, and our Universe some even larger entity. Our galaxy could be a molecule somewhere in the finger of a giant or on the hoof of a humongous horse, those huge objects each being the equivalent of a universe.

You get the idea.

A light-year is an unimaginably huge distance to us—six trillion miles—but it's an impractically small measure when considering some of the distances beyond our galaxy. I'm going to suggest a larger unit of measure called the "Nielsen" (hey, I invented it, so I get to name it!). It's the equivalent of a million light-years. That makes the diameter of the Milky Way $1/10^{th}$ of a Nielsen, the distance to the next closest galaxy one Nielsen, and the size of the Universe 91 thousand Nielsens.

See how much more manageable those numbers are?

Our Universe is expanding, that is, the galaxies are moving farther apart. If the Universe is part of a living, *growing* organism, that would explain everything.

An Endless Chain

British philosopher and Nobel Prize winner Bertrand Russell gave a lecture in 1927 and got interrupted by a feisty, older lady questioning his explanation on the construction of the Universe. She didn't believe the Earth was round and orbited the Sun. Unable to convince her, he asked for her opinion on the subject.

"The Earth is flat and it's on the back of a turtle," she claimed. Thinking he could trap her, Russell asked what the turtle was standing on. "It's turtles all the way down!" she replied.

That woman and I are kindred spirits in that we both believe there are continuous conglomerations of atoms and solar systems, galaxies and molecules, universes and finite beings, and that these conglomerations go both directions, getting larger and smaller.

Bertrand Russell

Evolution or Intelligent Design

As mentioned earlier, I have only to think about the size our Universe to realize what a minor role I play in the scheme of things. Evolution Theory posits that our world was created by chance, but Albert Einstein famously declared that God does not play dice, that chance is impossible in nature.

I agree with Einstein (brilliant minds think alike), but I'm not going to argue with folks who hold differing opinions. I probably couldn't persuade them anyway.

So, what do I believe?

I think our World *had* to be created by design. I just don't see how all this stuff could have happened via an improbable series of coincidences. If our world is a fluke of nature, that would mean I'm even less important than I think I am and that I have no real purpose. I try to keep my ego under control, but I just can't make it *that* small.

Yes, I'm an unrepentant Intelligent Design subscriber. I think He put this whole thing together, just as it says in the Good Book. Nothing else makes sense to me. I think the World is about eight thousand years old, as stated in the Bible, and not billions of years old as claimed by many scientists.

Okay, but what about dinosaurs and other prehistoric creatures? They've got to be much older than eight thousand years, don't they?

When God created the World, He also created a "history" of the World. He created fossils and other "evidence" of things thousands, millions, or even billions of years old. I don't think He would have created the entire world with everything in it appearing to originate on the same date.

That's what I think happened. My theory reconciles everything in my mind, allowing me to explain everything I see, as well as things scientifically "proven" to have happened in the past.

I'm comfortable with my theory. What's yours?

Incidentally, I've got some strong support for my theory. Hugh Ross is an astrophysicist at Cal Tech and he's written several books on the subject, among them *Why the Universe Is the Way It Is*, in which he reconciles Intelligent Design with science. My theory and his are mostly simpatico.

How it *Didn't* Happen

Charles Darwin may have been the first to develop and espouse the theory of natural selection as the vehicle that originated and developed life on Earth. He said that the correct elements just happened to bump into each other in some primordial pool and—*voila!*—life resulted. From that original and accidental life form, it eventually morphed into something else, and that something morphed again, until we have the myriad of living organisms now present on Earth.

Many modern scientists agree with Darwin's theory; they just can't imagine how He was able to wave a wand or declare life to be, and then have it happen. Looking carefully, such scientists seem to ignore one of the cornerstones of scientific reason, The Second Law of Thermodynamics, which states: Entropy in a closed system tends to stay the same or get worse.

Entropy is a scientific word for disorder, and a closed system is a structure that has not been influenced by an intelligent being.

If life originated as posited by scientists in direct conflict with this law, then here are a few examples of other events that should have occurred:

- A tornado should have hit an auto junk yard and left in its wake a complete and functional Cadillac Escalade
- An earthquake should have jumbled a backyard pile of bricks and mortar, leaving behind a fully assembled barbecue pit

Nothing like those things has ever happened, even though each would be much simpler and more likely than the accidental creation of life.

So, what are the odds against the accidental creation of life?

Getting back to Bill Bryson's book, in *A Short History of Nearly Everything* he calculates that the chances of this happening are one in a zillion.

I just made up "zillion." What Bryson really said was that to create life you'd need to combine 1055 different amino acids in exactly the right amounts and sequence. The chances of that happening by accident, he tells us, are nil; it just isn't going to happen. For the mathematically inclined he says the chances of this occurring would be on the order of one in 1×10^{260}. For the less mathematically inclined, 1×10^{260} would be the number one followed by 260 zeros. For perspective, that's a number larger than the number of atoms in the entire universe.

For the sake of argument, let's stipulate that such a long shot did come to pass. What would we have?

That first life form had to be a plant. Animals eat plants or other animals, but there weren't any, so the first life form couldn't have been an animal because it would have starved to death and that would have been the end of life on Earth.

On the other hand, a plant could survive on nutrients from the sun and soil.

Stipulating again that the first life form was a plant, where did animals come from?

Mutating from a plant to an animal just doesn't seem likely at all, so there must have been another astronomical long shot to create another life form, this one an animal. The odds against all this happening are increasing exponentially. Additionally, the animal would have had to be a vegetarian (no meat available), and it would have to be hermaphroditic to reproduce. Now we're really talking about even more astronomical long shots, probably one chance in $1\text{x}10^{260}$ *times* $1\text{x}10^{260}$. That'd be $1\text{x}10^{260\text{x}260}$, or a one followed by 67,500 zeros. So, if you were betting at the two-dollar window…

All of this blows the Second Law of Thermodynamics to smithereens, but it's the only way the scientific community can rationalize life on this planet, as unlikely as it must seem to them.

So, let's review the probabilities of Darwinism:

1. Despite tremendous odds, all 1055 of the required amino acids just happened to fall together in exactly the correct sequence and amounts to create life.
2. That life had to be a plant because there was no food available for an animal. That requirement raised the odds astronomically.
3. The original plant reproduced and morphed into other plants until we have the complete spectrum of flora now present on Earth, but those plants couldn't morph into an animal.

4. Despite tremendous odds, all 1055 of the required amino acids just happened to fall together in exactly the correct sequence and amounts (again!) to create an animal.

5. That animal had to be a vegetarian (no meat available) and it had to be hermaphroditic to reproduce. Once more, the odds of all this happening increased dramatically.

6. That animal, whatever it was, morphed into other animals until we have the complete plethora of fauna now present on the Earth.

7. Or were there other miraculous longshots in that primordial pool to create other life forms?

To quote Sir Arthur Conan Doyle in one of his Sherlock Holmes stories, "When you have eliminated the impossible, whatever remains, however improbable, must be the truth."

In the analysis above, we've eliminated Darwinism as impossible. Despite skepticism from the scientific community, however improbable, Intelligent Design is the only remaining possibility, so it must be the truth.

The Bible explains exactly what happened, but scientifically-minded folks just can't get their head around a supernatural Being creating life by simple declarations: "Let there be light. Let there be life. Etc.," but it's all right there in the book of Genesis.

ON EXERCISING

A friend of mine told me of a married couple who visited him at his home. When they were ready to leave, they had a tough time getting up off the couch and then shuffled unsteadily to the front door. My friend said he immediately thought of me, since I was about the same age as his guests. He knew I exercised regularly and thought the contrast in conditioning between me and his guests was startling.

I exercise regularly and plan to continue until I meet my Maker. I don't think I'll live forever, although it looks promising so far. My goal is to keep my quality of life as high as possible for as long as possible, rather than being physically limited, couch-bound, or (heaven forbid!) bedridden for years.

Use it or Lose it

I had some friends who were exercise fanatics, despite their advanced ages. They participated in several forms of vigorous exercise every day. They swam, ran, walked, played ping pong—sorry, I'm panting just thinking about all the things they did. They often said, "Use it or lose it!"

I visited them at their apartment one evening and rang the doorbell to gain entrance. The gentleman had to come down from an upper floor to open the door—no remote buzzer. After letting me in, he bounded up the steps, two at a time. At the top, he turned and admitted, "I'm just showing off!" The gentleman was 96 years old.

I hope to be just like him when I get that old. Oops, too late—I can't take the stairs two at a time today! But I'll keep doing whatever I can for as long as I can.

I've got a cousin who retired a few years ago. During his career, he was a physical dynamo who worked 16-hour days, sometimes much more. But once he retired, he *retired*. He seldom gets up off the couch and can barely walk when he does. What a sudden and total deterioration. Such a shame. Don't let it happen to you.

Getting Started

If you aren't already on an exercise regimen, see a doctor to learn if you have any limitations for exercise. Tell him what exercises you'd like to do, and then ease into the ones your doctor approves. If you're going to walk, jog, or whatever, begin slowly. Then increase the intensity and time very gradually, no more than 10 percent per week.

Another friend of mine (yup, I have more than one) went for his annual checkup and the doctor asked him how much exercise he got. My friend told him that he bowled, golfed, and played softball. The doctor wrote on my friend's chart: NO EXERCISE!

Many experts recommend at least 30 minutes of aerobic exercise at least three times a week—once a week is worse than not exercising at all due to an elevated risk of heart attack. Bowling and golf offer little aerobic exercise. You'll get some sporadic aerobics if you walk the golf course, almost none if you ride a cart. Softball might provide five minutes total aerobics over the course of a game, but too fragmented to do much good. A good, fast walk would be much better, if it lasted at least 30 minutes. Jogging would be good, too, if that's your thing. Devices like treadmills, stair-steppers, stationary bikes, or elliptical trainers are also a good way to get your heart rate up and exercise your muscles.

If you decide to take up walking or running (especially running), be sure to wear good shoes and dress appropriately. Avoid cement streets and sidewalks, as the shock to your joints is heavy. Asphalt is better, it has a little give, but grass or dirt is best. You might want to avoid uneven surfaces, such as trails, especially if you have ankle or knee problems. School tracks or ball fields are ideal.

Avoid shoes that have little or no arch support, and if you're running avoid department store knockoffs that look just like running shoes but aren't. Stick to known brands that are designed specifically for running. Think of your running shoes as an investment, not an expense.

Don't use your running shoes for mowing the lawn or walking the mall. Other activities break in shoes differently than running and could lead to injuries. Have an idea of how many miles you have on a pair of running shoes. Once you get up to 500, it's time for a new pair—support and cushioning don't last much longer than that. For example, if you run an average of 10 miles per week, that's about 500 miles per year and time for a new pair. Once you retire a pair of running shoes, they'll still look good and be just fine for mowing the lawn or strolling the mall.

Whether walking or running, you'll need to dress appropriately. I love the new, microfiber dri-fit clothing that has come out in recent years. It's light and it breathes. On warmer days, it'll wick moisture away from your skin; on cooler days, it'll keep you warm. It's magic!

On cool days, you'll need to wear several loose, thin layers of clothing, rather than one thick layer. There's an insulating air space between thin layers to keep you warmer than one thick layer. Also, you should be just a little cool at the start of your run or walk but be comfortable after about 10 minutes. If you're comfortable at the start, you'll be sweating in 10 minutes—not a good thing on a cool day.

Once you're done with your aerobic exercises, some strength training would be good. Pump a little iron, do some pushups or sit-ups, or something else to tone up those muscles and strengthen your core.

Warning: Do not hold your breath when exerting yourself, as when lifting a heavy weight. To do so puts tremendous stress on the veins and arteries in your head and could lead to aneurisms.

Aren't you glad you read this book?

If losing a little lard is your goal, I'd recommend exercise along with dieting. Dieting by itself does nothing to eliminate the fat inside your body, especially around the heart.

Dieting alone may make you look better on the outside, but you may not be any healthier on the inside.

You don't have to run marathons or be an Olympic weightlifter to stay fit but do *something*. Here are a few pearls from folks you may want to emulate:

- *"As you grow older, if you don't move, you won't move."* 88-year-old figure skater Yvonne Dowlen
- *"You just don't let that rocking chair take over. You get up and do something even if you don't want to."* 102-year-old cowgirl Constance Reeves

ON RESTAURANTS

My wife and I love dining out. We love great restaurants, not necessarily expensive ones. We treat ourselves infrequently to a high-priced meal, but usually go to reasonably priced places that have good food and service.

Buffets

We go to restaurants featuring buffets, but not too often. Years ago, we went to one and, before getting any food, my wife went to the restroom. As she walked into the lavatory, another lady came out of one of the stalls, walked right past the sinks, and out the door without washing her hands. By the time my wife had completed her ablutions, she came out of the lavatory and noticed the aforementioned lady at the buffet handling the spoons, forks, and other utensils.

My wife decided we would order off the menu that evening!

Maybe cleaning our hands *after* using the buffet and before eating would avoid the problem of other people's unsanitary habits.

Public Restrooms

While we're on the subject, public restrooms often have an obnoxious odor, usually caused by folks failing to flush the fixtures. That's probably why the engineers came up with self-flushing commodes and urinals. An infrared sensor detects the arrival of a human body, and when the body leaves the sensor triggers the flushing mechanism. Presto, no more stinky restroom.

I recall the first time I ran across one of those innovations. I was on a business trip and making a plane change in Dallas. While waiting for my plane Mother Nature called, advising me that I was about to have a moving experience. I quickly availed myself of the nearest sanitary facilities.

When I finished and bent over to do the paperwork, the commode erupted like Mount Vesuvius. When I tell you the toilet flushed, I mean to tell you it *flushed!* I got drenched from knees to waist. Picture the bidet from Hell or a busted fire hydrant. My only option was to leap out of Old Faithful's line of fire. I used three rolls of tissue paper to dry off my posterior. Luckily, I wore a dark suit that day so no one could see how wet it was. However, for an hour or two I knew just how soggy my undershorts were.

There are almost always bugs to be worked out in new technology. In this case the infrared detector sensitivity needed adjusting and the commode water pressure needed to be reduced quite a bit. I unwittingly served as a beta tester.

Tipping

Wait staff normally get a very low hourly wage, depending on tips to make up the difference. That would motivate most wait staff to excel so they can earn big bucks. Good service earns a 20 percent tip from us and great service can earn even more. We usually tip less, around 10 percent, at self-serve restaurants, like buffets.

Naturally, borderline service doesn't do quite so well. I recall one waitress who was downright rude to us. When we signed our credit card bill, we included a five-cent tip, just so she'd know we didn't forget her. You should have seen the look on the manager's face when he saw that. I'm sure our waitress got the message. We haven't seen her at that restaurant since then, so maybe management got the message, too.

Rating Service

So, what constitutes marginal service, aside from rudeness?

One of my pet peeves is wait staff who bring the succeeding course while we're still working on the previous one (e.g., bringing the entrées while we're still eating our salads). One waiter brought out our appetizers, soups, salads, and entrées on the same tray and, while placing them in front of us, asked if we'd like dessert! Okay, I'm exaggerating, but not by much.

While on a tour of Ireland many years ago, we noticed that the wait staff did not bring succeeding courses, not even beverages, until we asked for them. We thought that was very civilized, but it'd never play in Peoria. Diners in this country are often in a hurry and don't want to sit around doing nothing. Meanwhile, the wait staff is anxious to turn over their tables to new diners to maximize tip potential. We're in a hurry, they're in a hurry, it works out well for all.

We're not in favor of four-hour meals either, but we don't want the entrée getting cold while we finish our salad.

I often advise the wait staff of such preferences when ordering.

Speaking of wait staff, have you noticed that many of them refer to everyone at your table as "guys," even if there are ladies present?

My wife would never be mistaken for a guy, even by the most unobservant waiter. There must be a training institute somewhere that teaches wait staff to call everyone guys because we've seen it at some better restaurants, not just greasy spoons. I've overheard wait staff addressing a table of all females as guys. I don't like wait staff calling even a tableful of men guys. I've never let it affect my tipping habits, but I'm not in favor of this. That's just a bit too informal for me, but maybe I'm an old fuddy-duddy.

ON THE VIETNAM WAR

There may not have been a more divisive event in the history of the United States. Our country, communities, and even families were split over whether we should be fighting in Vietnam. There were riots and demonstrations daily. Newspaper, radio, and TV pundits told us what we ought to think about it; some supported the war effort, but most were against it. I'm somewhere in between.

Yes or No
We were a signatory to the Southeast Asia Treaty Organization, a pact wherein we promised to help protect and defend other signatory countries. That committed us to help South Vietnam fight off aggression by North Vietnam.

Some argued the South had a corrupt government. Or, they're just one country way over there and we shouldn't be involved. And finally, Vietnam is Vietnam—so what if the North wants to take over the South?

If the United States happened to elect a corrupt government (some would say it's happened more than once already!), should Canada or Mexico attack and try to take us over?

If we thought South Vietnam had a corrupt government, we could have used diplomatic means to steer them in the right direction. Overthrowing their government should have been a last resort and allowing another country to conquer them shouldn't have been an option at all.

Now That We're There
Once we made the decision to assist the South, we should have pulled out all stops. If we ever get into another war, we should end it as quickly as possible. To do otherwise is to maximize our loss of lives and resources. Over 58 thousand American soldiers gave their lives and an untold number were wounded during the Vietnam War, while expending trillions of dollars in resources.

That war could have been resolved quickly, certainly in less than a year. Instead, President Johnson and Secretary of Defense McNamara opted to run the war from the White House, seldom giving much consideration to the input from military commanders. Military commanders should not be given a free reign, but neither should they be ignored—they understand military tactics and they're on the ground where the rubber meets the road, while the politicians are in their Ivory Tower… er…White House.

Johnson, McNamara, and McNamara's advisors (euphemistically called The Whiz Kids) favored a flexible response strategy, as opposed to the Eisenhower doctrine of massive retaliation. McNamara believed by exerting pressure and stepping it up gradually, they'd eventually bring the North to its knees.

I'm with Ike. I think they should have hit the North immediately with everything we had. Let them know right off the bat they had no chance. Bludgeon them into submission.

Instead, Johnson and McNamara had our troops fight to conquer objective after objective. For example, they'd order our troops to take Hill 805, and our troops would do just that. After a week or two of fierce battle and many casualties on both sides, the enemy would withdraw. And so would we! Aerial reconnaissance a day or two later would report that Hill 805 looked like an anthill; the enemy was back in force. A month or so hence, the White House would order our troops to retake Hill 805. The troops had to be thinking, *Oh no, not again!*

One of the primary concepts of successful war strategy is to conquer terrain and then keep it. Letting the enemy have it back makes no sense whatever.

Rules of Engagement
The Ho Chi Minh Trail was a source of great controversy. The North Vietnamese used it as a supply route from North Vietnam, through Laos and Cambodia, down to South Vietnam. The Whiz Kids' Rules of Engagement (ROE) forbade any US forces from going outside South Vietnam. It didn't take the North long at all to figure that out. They soon knew they could move entire convoys of troops and supplies along the Ho Chi Minh Trail without fear of attack. At the end of the Trail, they'd break down the supplies and troops who then would disperse into the South. Had our side been allowed to bomb the convoys before they dispersed, many battles could have been avoided and many American lives saved. Instead, they had to fight many smaller battles with newly armed enemy combatants.

A Marine tank company came under attack from across a river. A private cranked up his tank and swung the main gun around to return fire, but his commander flipped the master switch to shut down the tank. Incensed, the private went to the company commander to report his tank commander. The company commander, a captain, told the private, "Son, you're lucky the lieutenant did what he did. Otherwise, you'd be facing a court martial."

Firing across that river would have violated the Whiz Kids' ROE. The tank company couldn't even defend itself from enemy fire. Again, arbitrary rules rather than sound battle tactics ruled the day. Such ROE had to be a morale killer for our troops, not to mention a literal killer.

Once We Left

In 1973, President Nixon and Secretary of State Henry Kissinger negotiated "peace with honor," whatever that is. The plan was for us to withdraw all our troops but to continue supplying the South with such things as arms and ammunition to successfully continue the war on their own. However, Congress saw fit to defund that initiative immediately. The result was predictable: The North soon overran the South, killing many and enslaving the rest.

Completely abandoning a SEATO ally is not my idea of honor.

ON FIGHTING TO WIN

If you're in a bar fight and insist on observing Marquis de Queensbury Rules, someone will hit you with a pool cue or a chair, and you'll lose in a hurry. A wag once said, "If you fight fair, your tactics suck!"

Terrorism
We should be tolerant of any religion known to man, except for a few radical sects that aren't religions at all. That would include some radical Islamic sects. No legitimate religion would promote annihilation or subjugation of all infidels. That concept is no different from that of Adolf Hitler or Genghis Khan.

And it's such a shame. Folks in southwest Asia and northern Africa led the world in advances in such areas as astronomy and mathematics. Then in the seventh century Muhammed came along and, aside from weapons improvisation and assault tactics, all progress ceased never to resume.

Radical Islam may be the most restrictive "religion" in the history of the world. Followers not only try to annihilate or subjugate non-Muslims, they're very intolerant of other

Muslims who don't practice their exact beliefs. Radical Muslims say it's their way or the die-way. Additionally, all women are treated as chattel who have no rights whatever. And don't even ask about gays!

Mysterious Mindset

Though treated as chattel, many Muslim women subscribe to hardline beliefs. For example, a retired nurse, a Jewish lady, spoke at our church one evening. She said that since retiring she's done volunteer work, including a trip to the Middle East.

While there, she worked in a hospital maternity ward. One day a Muslim woman gave birth to a boy, the first male born into the family. She asked the nurse if she'd pray with her and give thanks. The nurse said she'd be honored and they both knelt by the bed.

"Bless Allah for giving me a healthy baby boy," the new mother began. "May he grow up strong and kill many Jews as a suicide bomber."

That's hardline!

In Appendix A of David Hunt's book, *They Just Don't Get It*, is an excerpt from the Koran. Among the chilling directives therein is this: "Smile at the infidel with you face, but never with your heart. The infidel must not know what you have in store for him until it is too late." In other words, be deceptive, very deceptive, until the infidel is totally off guard and then you can kill or subjugate him.

Now that's hardline!

Many politicians declare, "Islam is a religion of peace," but an infidel needs to wonder, how many Muslims subscribe to this directive. Is it just the Wasabi's and other more radical sects, or is it all of Islam?

The Solution

So, how do we eliminate this problem?

Radical Muslims (at least) are bent on annihilating everyone who doesn't believe *exactly* as they do, even less radical Muslim sects. They've been trying to do that for 1400 years and it won't stop until one side or the other is history. Meanwhile, they'll target mostly civilians, even children. If they've blown up, say, a nursery, they'll rush to the media to "take responsibility" for the heinous act.

Many in our power structure warn us not to overreact when something like this happens. We see just how well that works. If someone slaps you, slapping him back will elicit a punch or kick in return. What needs to happen is not a proportional response, but an overwhelming one. Overreacting is exactly what is needed to stop an assault; hit them at least twice as hard as they've hit you.

Radical Muslims are not American citizens, or if they are should not be granted the rights of a citizen. Anyone who declares war or performs aggression against the United States should forfeit all legal guarantees.

Politicians a few years ago wanted to bring captured combatants to New York city for trial. What a circus that would have been. Those terrorists would have loved that platform to declare their hatred of the US. Also, much of the evidence against them is very sensitive and should not be presented in open court; that's what military tribunals are for.

We've got to keep after terrorists militarily. We'll have a tough time wiping them out completely, but we've got to try. While we're doing that, radical jihadists can't get too offensive if they're busy playing defense fulltime.

I think the final answer is education.

Guys like Osama bin Laden didn't fly planes into the World Trade Center. Neither did they strap bombs to themselves and blow up subways. They had their ignorant followers do that. If the followers weren't ignorant in the first place, it might have occurred to them they were doing their leaders' bidding, but their leaders never had any skin in the game.

Another possibility is to put the fear of God in terrorists. That may not seem possible since they seem to relish the possibility of death, believing they'll go instantly to Jannah (Islamic heaven) where they'll each be ministered to by 72 virgins.

The one thing they seem to fear, their silver bullet if you will, is a pig. There's an unconfirmed rumor that back in the early part of the 20th century there were Muslim terrorists wreaking havoc in the Philippines. US General John "Black Jack" Pershing and his men captured a few terrorists alive. He had several pigs slaughtered in front of the captives. His men then dipped the tips of many bullets into the pigs' blood. Then the men executed all but one of the terrorists, shooting them with the tainted ammunition. They shoved the bodies of the dead terrorists into a large hole, then dumped the pig carcasses in, too, before filling the hole with dirt. And finally, they released the one living terrorist, who, terrified, fled and spread the word to his fellow terrorists. The legend declares there was no further Muslim terrorism in the Philippines for 50 years.

That urban legend can't be proven or disproven, but something along those lines could work. The US should announce publicly that we've developed a way of making ammunition that involves using pig blood or some such. Realizing that likely jihadists may not have access to TV, radio, or newspapers, we could use drones to drop leaflets in likely terrorist territories, declaring that all munitions used by the US will heretofore be tainted. Additionally, any dead terrorists or terrorist body parts will be interred using porcine products.

I'm sure there'd be a hue and cry from the jihadists and even from some people vulnerable to terrorism, both in this country and abroad. For that last group, political correctness trumps national safety. We need to decide if we're going to be bound by political correctness or whether we're more interested in survival. We can't have it both ways.

Most of this chapter so far was originally in the On Religion chapter; I think you can see why I moved it. Radical Islam really isn't a religion.

Waterboarding

The United States no longer waterboards captured enemy combatants. We're told we should be above that, that we should set the example on how to conduct war in a dignified manner.

Senator John McCain was an American hero, no doubt about it, but he was wrong on this subject. He was a prisoner of the North Vietnamese for several years. He was treated inhumanely and should know what real torture is, but maybe he endured too much of it and lost his perspective. He declares that waterboarding is cruel and unusual punishment, and any intelligence gathered is unreliable anyway.

Many other politicians with lesser knowledge said the same thing, but evidence proves them wrong. If waterboarding truly is ineffective, there wouldn't be so many countries who use the technique.

Khalid Sheikh Mohammed was the principal architect of the 9/11 attack. He was subsequently captured and sent to

Guantanamo Bay where he was interrogated and—wait for it—waterboarded. Leading up to waterboarding, Mohammed was utterly defiant and uncooperative. "You'll soon know what our plans are," he sneered. "By then it'll be too late." After waterboarding, Mohammed spilled his guts and we were able to avert many subsequent attacks.

Waterboarding is very productive and causes no lasting effects, psychological or otherwise. We put some of our own military personnel through the procedure, just so they'll know what they're dealing with. We wouldn't pull out anyone's fingernails (the enemy would), and waterboarding is nothing in comparison. If politicians who oppose waterboarding knew the enemy planned to annihilate their family, their stance probably would change so the needed information needed to save their family could be extracted.

A Level Playing Field

When we're involved in a war we need the fortitude to take out the enemy wherever they are. Our current foes, radical Muslims, take advantage of us at every opportunity. They don't wear uniforms, typically mingle with civilians, and often establish headquarters in such places as schools, mosques, and hospitals. The enemy is very familiar with our ROE and know we're reluctant to engage them in those facilities.

When we're involved in a war, we need to engage the enemy wherever he may be. As stated earlier, arbitrary ROEs hamstring our efforts and put our troops at a severe disadvantage, not to mention extreme danger. While we'd prefer not to attack schools, mosques, and hospitals, if that's where the enemy is, so be it. Don't think for a minute that they'd be reluctant to attack if our troops were in any of those places. If we're prohibited or even tentative about doing so, we're setting ourselves up for failure.

Will the press scream?

Of course, they will, but they know even less than politicians about how to conduct a war successfully. If we let the press tell us how to wage war, we're doomed.

In all wars there is collateral damage. While we wouldn't intentionally attack a civilian target (though terrorists often do), if there's a weapons cache in a mosque or a rocket battery on the first floor of a hospital, all bets are off. We should try to minimize collateral damage but achieving our objective—annihilation of the enemy—must take precedence. Otherwise, we're toast. Recall that we bombed places like Dresden and Hiroshima in WWII where collateral damage was heavy. We need to adopt the same mindset in modern warfare.

If we're involved in a war, we should be in it to win it, not be hamstrung by arbitrary rules devised by politicians who have no relevant knowledge and no skin in the game.

The Element of Surprise

In any kind of fight, you'll be much more successful if you don't telegraph your punches. If your opponent knows what's coming, he'll try to get out of the way and probably throw an effective counterpunch.

That applies especially in war. You should never declare your intentions, such as *We're going to bomb the Poobah's palace at 0800 tomorrow*. You may be successful in bombing the palace, although the Poobah's defenses should be on high alert and you might get blown up yourself. You can bet the Poobah himself will be elsewhere.

That's one of the risks of allowing embedded reporters in a tactical unit. All reporters are looking for a big scoop, to get the story out before anyone else does. Thus, they're prone to announce things that should not yet be for public consumption. That endangers our troops and jeopardizes their mission. Either embedded reporters shouldn't be allowed, or they shouldn't be privy to sensitive information about upcoming events.

Reporters and some politicians might insist the public has a right to know. No, they don't, not until the event is over. Successful combat operations and personnel safety should be the priority.

Exit Strategy

Lately, whenever we enter a conflict, someone will pose the question, "What is our exit strategy?"

Our exit strategy should be:

-We're in it to win it; we'll exit when the enemy is annihilated and unable to resist
- We don't announce a withdrawal date until hostilities have ended
- We don't declare victory; we keep fighting until the enemy declares defeat

If we're going to war at all, there should be no quarter given. Any potential enemy must know that when we enter a conflict, we will do all we can to win decisively and quickly.

Announcing a date of withdrawal before hostilities have ended benefits the enemy and no one else. The enemy will just hide and run out the clock. Once we've left the field of conflict, the enemy will reassert itself and we'll be right back where we started—or worse.

Politicians serve a useful purpose, but sometimes get overly involved in military operations. They should have a say but must thoughtfully consider recommendations from military commanders. The latter are aware of what is needed to secure victory while minimizing risks to our combat personnel. Politicians should be a tempering influence on overzealous military commanders, but they should not hamstring effective and necessary military operations.

We've had several conflicts in recent history (e.g., Vietnam) where lack of resolve and counterproductive ROE resulted in drawn-out campaigns that wasted time, national resources, and human life. That must not happen again.

ON RACE RELATIONS

I don't consider myself a racist and hope you find no reason to disagree once you've finished reading this chapter. I offer that caveat because I'm a white guy and I often feel I'm hated by some blacks because of it. I try not to be too resentful, just brush it off, but it's tough sometimes.

Reverse Discrimination

Let me tell you a little about my background. I grew up in rural Iowa. Aside from the train conductor passing through the area twice a day, there were no blacks within 50 miles. My teachers all the way through public school hammered racial equality into us, and the lesson took. We felt bad for what had happened to blacks in the past.

My dad grew up in Denmark—no blacks lived there. My mom grew up where I did—no blacks lived there. My mom's ancestors came from Germany in the 1800s—no blacks lived there. When I left high school for the big city I was the first in my extended family to have any interactions with blacks. I certainly did nothing to discriminate against them.

So, why do some of them hate me so much?

I've met blacks I'd never seen before who gave me looks of pure loathing. Some have gone out of their way to be physically intimidating. Others were rude behind the wheels of their automobiles; for example, a car in front of me stopped at a red light, sat there until it turned yellow, and then eased through the intersection leaving me sitting as it turned red. The color of my skin had to be the reason.

Assuming I'm not the only one to receive such treatment, blacks are hindering the advancement of their cause—being rude to the opposition isn't likely to elicit sympathy and co-operation from them.

However, if dissing me somehow makes those folks feel better about themselves, I guess I can live with it.

I spent most of my career in the Atlanta area, arguably the home of the civil rights movement. When Martin Luther King, Jr. passed away, other black pastors in the area fell all over each other trying to become the next MLK. Spinning the AM dial on the way to church on Sunday mornings, I ran across quite a few of them spouting venom from the pulpit, stuff that would have made Jeramiah Wright and Louis Farrakhan proud. Very un-Christian stuff. They told their rapt congregations that "whitey" was the cause of all their problems.

From that it seems if there's ever a race war in this country, it'll probably start in Atlanta.

By whitey, I assumed they meant all white folks and that bothered me. That's racism pure and simple, and don't give me the tripe about minorities not being capable of racism. Declaring hatred of a person because of his skin color is racism, no matter who says it.

MLK

Getting back to Martin Luther King, Jr., I just can't get too excited about his legacy or his national holiday. I'm probably in the minority and I'm sure he did some good things, but I can't get past my initial impressions of the man.

I began my career in 1965, not long before MLK began his famous *tour de force*. I watched the reports of his many stops on TV, heard about them on the radio, and read about them in the newspaper. He declared that blacks wanted jobs, but the Welfare Program had kicked in a year or two before and I got the distinct impression that nearly everyone at his rallies was on Welfare, loved it, and wanted no part of gainful employment.

His tour involved cities like Philadelphia, Cleveland, Detroit, and St Louis. Along with jobs, MLK also preached non-violence, but as soon as he left those who had been at his rallies looted and burned the city. Some non-violence!

The clincher for me was that as he continued his tour the rhetoric didn't change. He, too, must have seen the TV reports, heard them on the radio, or read about it in the paper. Shouldn't it have dawned on him that he was *fostering* violence?

Apparently, it didn't. Thus, he's directly responsible for burning a swath across the country.

MLK a man of peace? Not in my mind!

Reparations

We occasionally hear talk of paying reparations to all black folks (many thousands of dollars per person, presumably) for the way their ancestors were treated. That money would come out of tax revenue, your money and mine.

The slave owners and Ku Klux Klan members of yore are all dead, and so are the blacks they tormented. So, we who've never discriminated against anyone should pay reparations to folks who've never been discriminated against?

That just doesn't compute. It's wrongheaded thinking or a scam to end all scams. I refuse to pay for my own father's racial indiscretions (he didn't have any), let alone someone else's.

Reparations promoters probably think the same as I do but figure, *It can't hurt to ask for reparations anyway. Who knows, some idiot group might cough up some coins for us. Stranger things have happened.*

Many years ago, a group of black militants invaded a huge church in an eastern city, interrupting the service to demand reparations from the mostly white congregation. The thugs were invited to come back the following Sunday, at which time the church presented them with a check for $100 thousand dollars. I'll bet the thugs were flabbergasted their scam had worked—I'll bet many parishioners were equally flabbergasted and probably switched churches as a result.

What do you suppose the militants did with the money?

If they ever pulled that scam again, it wasn't in the media (no longer news?). With such a resounding success, I'd have thought they'd visit at least one church a week.

I've never understood "white guilt" or any other kind unless a person really is guilty of something. The days of whipping boys passed centuries ago, and reparations is nothing but whipping someone for what someone else did.

If blacks are owed reparations, shouldn't they first atone for all the missionaries they ate? Just saying.

Affirmative Action

Folks who think much like the leaders of the church above have instigated affirmative action to correct past injustices. Many bad things happened in the past—slavery, discrimination, etc.—but it's too late to correct any of that. None of the folks on either side are here today and we all need to move on. Affirmative action is identical to reparations, in that it amounts to rewarding folks who were never discriminated against, to the detriment of folks who never discriminated against anyone.

Some organizations, especially the government, set aside jobs and contracts for minorities. Those set-asides are often failures because, aside from skin color, the awardees can't fulfill the requirements. Also, some minority contract bidders are fronts for non-minority firms trying to get around the race requirements. Jobs and contracts should be awarded to the most qualified people, regardless of race.

Colorblindness is good.

Some colleges have implemented a quota system for study programs with limited openings, like medical school. If a school has 100 openings in the upcoming term, 13 of those openings must be filled by blacks. Aside from that criterion, the school accepts the top undergraduates. If that includes at least 13 blacks (more is permissible), problem solved. If it doesn't, they dip into the second or even third 100 students to get enough blacks to fill their quota. If there were only 13 blacks applying, they take them all regardless of their class standing.

No telling how many better-qualified non-black students in the top 100 don't make it into med school because of the quota, and no telling how many blacks who aren't in the top 100 make it into med school only to flunk out. But at least the school administrators are proud of their actions; bet they never look at the results.

I suspect that some blacks in pre-med studies keep an eye on their ranking versus other blacks. If they're among the top 13, regardless of their overall ranking, they know they're in and maybe don't try too hard.

Personally, I wouldn't want a doctor who got into med school solely because of the color of his/her skin, no matter what color it was.

Medical school, or any college program with limited access, should be reserved for the best and brightest without regard to skin color. I'd hate to be an otherwise qualified student who wasn't accepted into med school because I was the wrong color, and I'd be embarrassed to be admitted based solely on the color of my skin.

The Civil War ended 150 years ago. Trying to atone for the crimes of the long dead will accomplish nothing positive.

Switching Sides

Many of our politicians, state and national, fiercely supported segregation. They fought tooth and nail against the Civil Rights Act of 1964. Once Congress got the law passed, those same politicians did an immediate about-face, declaring themselves the supporters and salvation of minorities.

President Johnson was the guiding force behind the Welfare Program, passed the same year. In an unguarded moment he said, "When I get this Welfare Program up and running, I'll have all them niggers (his word, not mine) voting for me until the cows come home."

And he was right!

Politicians who had been vehemently anti-black now promised to provide a monthly check, so long as recipients voted for them. Does the term "vote buying" come to mind?

Blacks must have thought, *Gee, why do they want to give me money? I've done nothing to earn it. But hey, I'll vote for the sucker just in case he can do what he says.*

And the politicians came through as promised. And the blacks came through as promised. Many blacks switched sides and became the most monolithic voting bloc in the country, not realizing or ignoring the fact they were voting against their own self-interests.

Let's spend a few minutes to analyze what those votes were worth, aside from ensuring seats for politicians.

The politicians who had filibustered racial equality legislation suddenly claimed to be champions of such, and their successors followed suit. In truth, those politicians are still enslaving blacks, just in a more insidious form. Many blacks who had been gainfully employed before Welfare arrived retired to the porch, no longer having to work for a check.

The poverty rate in black communities did go down a bit, but at what cost?

Black males were emasculated; Uncle Sam was now the family bread winner. In fact, some wives kicked their husbands out of the family entirely. There were several reasons for this. First, the wives would get a larger check, being a single head-of-household. Second, there'd be one less mouth to feed. Some wives would allow their husbands or boyfriends to come back every year or so, so they could get pregnant—Welfare checks went up with the number of dependents.

Talk about rewarding bad behavior! No wonder the black illegitimacy rate went up to 75 percent, about triple what it was before Welfare.

Work or Welfare

I lived in a Chicago suburb when all this began, and it seemed most blacks there were on Welfare. A friend had a job in a local factory when his company first began hiring blacks, and one of them began working right next to my buddy.

"How long you been doing this crap?" he asked. When my buddy replied he'd been at it 10 years, the black said, "I ain't doing this. I'm going back on Welfare."

My buddy never saw that black man again.

The Welfare program seemed to encourage even physically able blacks to go on the dole and stay there.

Welfare caused a ton of other problems that plague the black community to this day. Idle hands are the Devil's workshop, and that was never truer than in the black community. While many sat on the porch and did nothing, others became criminal entrepreneurs. They began dealing drugs or committing petty crimes, even committing felonies. Drug use among the newly idle also skyrocketed.

Inner city schools are a disaster in many cases. Students feel they're being held hostage for 12 years to learn things for which they'll never have any use. Some of them have no relatives, not even grandparents, who've ever held a regular job. They don't figure they will either, so why should they learn English and algebra and all that other stuff? None of that is needed to collect a Welfare check.

Parental support (usually singular) is nonexistent. They've never held a job themselves and don't figure their children will either. It's no wonder many inner-city schools have become combat zones. Students are held there against their will, exposed (notice I didn't say "learning") to subjects that are of no conceivable use to them.

The result of Welfare is that some truly needy people were helped, but many others got on the gravy train when they could have been contributors to society instead of burdens. Poverty went down slightly, but crime, illegitimacy, unemployment, and drug use went up. On average, the Welfare Program is the worst thing that ever happened to the black community. The political "champions" of blacks must know this, but apparently consider their reelection more important than fixing the problem.

If you subsidize a certain behavior, you can expect to get more of that behavior. Here's a trenchant observation from Ben Franklin that puts Welfare in its proper perspective:

> "I am for doing good to the poor, but…I think the best way of doing good to the poor, is not making them easy in poverty, but leading or driving them out of it. I observed…that the more public provisions were made for the poor, the less they provided for themselves, and of course became poorer. And, on the contrary, the less was done for them, the more they did for themselves, and became richer."

The Solution

To solve the problem, we need to limit Welfare Program access to those who are truly needy. Able-bodied people should be encouraged, coerced even, to seek gainful employment. If jobs just aren't available, a doubtful scenario, they should be required to do public service or something to earn a small "Workfare" check until they can find a regular job. Paying able-bodied people *not* to work has got to come to an end. It truly benefits no one; quite the opposite.

Unfortunately, there are some politicians who realize that 47 percent of the people in this country pay no income taxes. They figure they'd be invincible at the polls if they could just get that untaxed group up to 51 percent. In other words, they're in the business of getting reelected, regardless of what happens to the country or their constituents. If they can make that happen, we'll be at the mercy of a majority and in a democracy for all intents and purposes. That's the root of the problem.

BLM

Black Lives Matter first came to my attention in the aftermath of the 2014 episode in Ferguson, Missouri. Suddenly, there was a hue and cry about police targeting innocent black people. Okay, maybe there was a hue and cry before that, but BLM began a strongly organized effort to bring this "problem" to national attention.

BLM chose a very poor incident to use as a springboard because the black "victim" in this case was nowhere near innocent. Michael Brown was a thug who had just committed strong-arm robbery. A police officer, Darren Wilson, apprehended Brown minutes later as he strolled down the middle of the street. Brown immediately became belligerent and attacked the officer, trying to take away Wilson's pistol. Wilson sustained some minor injuries but won the tug-of-war and shot Brown during the struggle.

Wilson soon had to quit his job despite a justified shooting. Brown died at the scene and became an immediate *cause celebre* for BLM. "Hands up, don't shoot!" became their rallying cry. Brown never said any of those things. If he had, he would be alive today.

Getting past the Ferguson incident, does BLM have a valid case for police abuse of black people in general?

Black people compose 12 or 13 percent, about an eighth, of the total population in this country. BLM claims that police disproportionately use excessive force against blacks. There's no doubt that violent confrontations between police and blacks exceed 13 percent, but there are valid reasons for that. First, blacks commit more than 13 percent of the crimes in this country (over half the murders, for example), so the rate of confrontation with police naturally will be higher than their population percentage. Second, blacks like Michael Brown tend to be uncooperative, belligerent, and even aggressive when confronted by police. Because of that attitude many officers are on edge when making a stop, sometimes causing them to overreact.

Racial Agitators

There are race hustlers and poverty pimps in this country who constantly tell blacks that whitey is out to get them, especially police. These despicable human beings cater to the poor and disenfranchised, not to improve the lot of the downtrodden but to line their own purses. They encourage the poor blacks to stay on Welfare, don't get a job, and to hate whitey and anyone successful. Ironically, "whitey" in their invective includes black policemen.

This inaccurate indoctrination instills in many blacks the notion that police are not their friends. Oddly, blacks at all levels of society are susceptible to this tripe. For example, a few years ago a black Harvard professor accidentally locked himself out of his own house. Police apprehended him trying to climb in a back window. That episode should have amounted to nothing, but the professor immediately became belligerent. The police cuffed the professor, took him to the station, and booked him. The problem got straightened out but would not have been a problem at all had the professor been cooperative; the police, after all, were just trying to protect the professor's own interests.

Are there instances where police overreact when confronting blacks?

Fortunately, police brutality is nearly non-existent, probably no higher against blacks than it is against any other race.

A few years back, there was a viral video showing a black man running away from a Charleston, South Carolina, policeman and the policeman emptying his pistol into the fleeing man's back. The victim died, and the policeman is now serving a long stretch in prison. I have no idea how the black man might have contributed to the incident, if at all, but it's hard to imagine how anyone could justify shooting an unarmed, fleeing person.

Fortunately, incidents like this are rare. They're just cases of an officer of the law doing bad things and, since such unusual occurrences have racial overtones, command the media spotlight; had the victim been a white man, we may never have heard of the incident.

It's too bad a man died, but good that his murderer got the justice he deserved.

Avoiding Police Confrontations
Regardless of your skin color, when approached by an officer of the law, do nothing to escalate a potentially volatile situation. Be respectful: "Yes officer." "No officer." Keep your hands in plain sight and obey all commands. If you need to reach for such things as identification or your phone, ask permission and if received move your hands slowly to retrieve the object. Cooperate with the officer to the best of your ability. Innocent or guilty, these guidelines will minimize the chance of an officer's overreaction.

Even how a person dresses can make a difference. Many stickup artists and other criminals choose to wear hoodies to minimize the chance of identification. Witnesses may not be able to identify even skin color unless they get a head-on view of the culprit.

Consequently, police notice a person wearing a hoodie, especially if he's wearing the hood up in July. While such dress may be trendy, it could also attract police attention who might suspect a person dressed thusly has committed a crime or is about to. At the very least, an officer might suspect the hoodie wearer of carrying a firearm, drugs, or contraband; that's what criminals often wear.

"Harassment!" many would cry.

But looking like a criminal could get you treated like one. Someone wearing a mask would certainly draw some attention and wearing a hoodie is not that far removed; both are common criminal garb.

A person who gets stopped and questioned might be inconvenienced for about two minutes. If that person is innocent, he/she should shrug it off, realizing that the officer is making his/her neighborhood safer.

Unfortunately, many honest citizens can't see past the police harassment angle that many in their community trumpet. Rather than resenting the police, innocent citizens "stopped while driving Black" shouldn't blame the police. Rather, most of the blame should be attributed to the small number of black criminals who give the rest of their race a bad name.

I saw a black policeman recently, wearing a T-shirt that said, "I'm here to protect your ass, not kiss it." Remember, police officers really are our friends. Don't make it otherwise.

ON OUR ANTHEM

The *Star-Spangled Banner* is sung before many major events. It's a way of saluting our freedom, our military, our way of life, and many other things. It should be a solemn occasion, but some folks have used it to highlight different agendas.

The NFL Protest

My wife and I didn't watch any NFL game during the 2018 season. That was our response to some NFL players protesting police brutality against blacks by kneeling during the anthem. However, we did record the Super Bowl. The following evening, we watched all the commercials, fast-forwarding through the game itself.

We didn't really do that, but we thought about it.

We happened to be watching the evening news on another channel when the anchor reporter announced the Super Bowl had started and no one had refused to stand for the *Star-Spangled Banner*. My wife and I looked at each other and decided the players' protest must be over, so we could end ours, too. We watched the game, but quite a few folks didn't.

The next day we heard a report about the NFL *paying* the players to stand for the anthem, conceivably to put an end to the black eye the protestors were giving the league. If that's true, it raises suspicion about the players' true courage of their convictions. I'm hoping that's not true and the players finally wised up.

The protestors picked a rotten way of calling attention to their perceived problem. Most people in this country have a deep reverence for our flag and the *Star-Spangled Banner*. Refusing to honor the flag, the anthem, and our country rubbed a ton of people, probably most of them, the wrong way.

What would the protestors think if another group chose to protest an unrelated cause and chose disrespecting MLK Day to do it?

They wouldn't like it any more than we like their using our flag and anthem for their protest.

Guest Renditions

The national anthem is sung before sporting and other events and is supposed to be done in honor of our country and military. In the last 30 years or so, it's morphed into a chance for singers to showcase their vocal acrobatics.

The first performer I recall doing that was Jose Feliciano, I think for a World Series game. Since then, stylized renditions have become the norm and many people resent it. They're impressed only by folks who can sing a song *exactly* as written. To do otherwise makes them suspect the "artist" just can't follow a score, maybe can't even read music, or is trying to show off.

One star sang the song so slowly that it was nearly halftime before she finished. Advertisers must have been tearing their hair out over all the missed ad spots.

Rossini, the great opera composer, had a similar problem with some of the folks who sang the arias he wrote; they'd add notes where he hadn't put them and didn't want them. That led Rossini to write arias so complex there just wasn't room for improvisation.

The *Star-Spangled Banner* has a fairly complex tune, but that doesn't stop some singers from personalizing it. I'd love to see some of these self-declared virtuosos under the baton of a stern conductor, someone like James Levine of the New York Metropolitan Opera. I'm sure he'd insist they follow the score to a tee; if they couldn't, he'd tell them to hit the bricks and he'd find someone who could.

Preceding a World Series game some years ago, a 13-year-old girl had been selected to do the honors, but she turned it into a disgrace. Her rendition was so stylized as to render the melody unrecognizable. During the song, the TV cameras panned the crowd and players, many of whom stared at the singer in utter disbelief. About halfway through the song, the singer herself didn't recognize the tune any-more. She stopped briefly and started over, this time follow-ing the score and sang it well. But when she got to the part where she'd lost her place, she resumed her butchery.

When she'd finished, play-by-play announcer Vin Scully complimented the girl for her recovery. I was just happy the agony had ended.

A singer at a recent event mutilated the tune so badly that players and fans were laughing uproariously. You had to wonder if she was stoned or otherwise impaired. She apol-ogized the following day, but most such artists don't have that much grace.

Back in the 1970s there was a baseball Game of the Week on TV every Saturday. The Reggie Jackson Yankees were the cocks of the walk in those days and were featured in many of those telecasts. Yankee Stadium usually had a famous singer perform the *Star-Spangled Banner* before each game. One Saturday there was a bit of a mix-up, declared the stadium announcer. He said two stars were in attendance, each intending to do the honors. Both graciously agreed to do a duet. Pop singer Jerry Vail was at the top of his game in those days, and Robert Merrill was a star at the Met. When they took the field to sing the song, Merrill blew Jerry Vail off the mound—what a powerful voice. As I said, Vail was excellent himself but just didn't have the pipes to match Merrill. Merrill probably could have filled the stadium without a PA system.

If you missed that performance, you missed a real treat. Unless you're a big fan of Jerry Vail.

For a modern-day rendition sure to please, tune in a Sunday Chicago Cubs home game. The stadium announcer, Wayne Mesmer, usually does the honors and nails it without fail. Occasionally, Mesmer's wife Kathleen will join him, and they'll sing a duet, Kathleen singing melody and her husband harmony. Even if you don't like baseball, I'd encourage you to tune in just for the national anthem. What a treat!

ON TV ADS

Some of the Super Bowl games have been very good and some not so good, but the commercials themselves are usually worth the four hours spent watching the watching machine. Vendors realize the Super Bowl will be the biggest audience they'll reach each year, so they pull out all the stops to make a good impression.

Some ads you won't see during a Super Bowl don't make a good impression when they do run. I'm speaking of ads for attorneys and ads for prescription medications.

Attorney Ads

Attorneys for the most part provide a valuable service we all need occasionally. But ads for attorneys reveal the ambulance chasers in this country. I can't recall a TV ad for attorney services that sounded like it came from a reputable firm. They all come across as shysters hoping to sue companies or individuals and force a settlement without having to go to trial. Easy money for bottom feeders, in other words.

Such shysters know defendants, even those who are blameless, might be willing to settle out of court rather than risk the bad publicity of a public trial, not to mention the possibility of a rogue jury finding a verdict against them. Lawyers know that if they don't sue for too much the defendant might settle out of court. The defendant also knows he might be wise to settle, even if he's innocent; attorney fees to defend court cases can be astronomical, sometimes more than a trial judgement.

I'd love to see a loser-pays law put into effect. That way, if a shyster brings a frivolous suit to court and loses, he would have to pay all defense and court costs. As it is now, shysters have a good chance of winning a settlement without going to court, and defendants have a monetary incentive to settle even if they're innocent. With a loser-pays law, innocent defendants could clear their names without incurring crippling expenses.

But lawyers can't make much money that way and lawyers make the laws, so don't hold your breath for tort reform.

Drug Ads

TV ads for prescription drugs are not in a consumer's best interest. They tout meds for a given malady and then suggest, "Ask your doctor if XYZ is right for you."

If your doctor is worth what you're paying him, he'll be up-to-date on the latest meds and will prescribe XYZ, if appropriate, without you prompting him. A patient suggesting meds might sway a marginal physician to prescribe certain drugs, and that's what pharmaceutical advertisers hope will happen. If you could influence your doctor into prescribing something you saw on TV, you should consider getting a different doctor.

Oh, how I long for the days before attorney and prescription medicine ads. We've advanced a long way in many areas, but these two are not among them.

ON DRUG PRICES

We often hear complaints about the cost of drugs and some of those costs can be astronomical, especially for cancer treatment and some other maladies. In most cases those prices are justified (you'll see why in the next paragraphs) and will come down with time. That may not be much consolation if you're undergoing cancer treatment right now.

Why Drug Prices Are So High

The cost to manufacture and distribute drugs usually isn't much. There's also the cost of promotion, such as sending representatives to visit physicians and placing ads on TV (wish those ads would curl up and die!). The real expense is in drug development. Five thousand failed attempts before developing one successful drug is about average. That's a ton of expense and needs to be recovered by the pharmaceutical manufacturer in the sale of the successful product.

Once a product has been approved by the Food & Drug Administration and goes on the market, the pharma can begin recouping some of its investment. For a while they may have cornered the market until their patent runs out. Until then, their new miracle drug rules the roost and they can charge whatever the market will bear.

However, pharma competitors will be anxious to get in on the boon. They may have to wait until the patent expires, or they may come up with a different formula that provides similar benefits. But if they expect to be competitive with the first pharma, they'll have to price their drug a bit lower. That will prompt the first pharma to drop its prices, too. It's called capitalism and the consumer wins.

Cheaper Drugs from Canada

We've all heard stories (some may be true) of people getting mail-order American drugs from another country for lower prices than can be found in the States. A patient should be leery of the quality of those drugs. If the drugs are authentic American-made drugs, there may be other reasons for this phenomenon.

Imagine a Chief Executive Officer and the Chairman of the Board of Directors at a big pharmaceutical company having the following conversation:

CEO: Boss, we've been contacted by the government of Lower Slobovia. They want to buy 100 million of our XYZ pills, but they only want to pay $2 per pill.

Chairman: What does it cost to manufacture and deliver XYZ?

CEO: About a buck a pill, but that leaves little room to recoup our research and development costs.

Chairman: What do our pills sell for in this country?

CEO: We get $10 per pill.

Chairman: Do we expect domestic sales to cover the cost of R&D?

CEO: Yes, we do.

Chairman: Then sale of the pills to Lower Slobovia

would result in a $1 per pill profit. Get back to them and seal the deal before they change their minds.

Pharmaceutical companies surely consider domestic *and* foreign sales when establishing the price on newly developed drugs, but if they hadn't included Lower Slobovia the above scenario is entirely possible and could explain how a foreign country could sell an American drug back to us cheaper than we can buy it here.

Universal Health Care

There's a frequent hue and cry in this country for universal health care, also called single payer. In that scenario, instead of a patient dealing directly or through an insurance company with his physician, a government agency would administer UHC.

Proponents decry that we're among the few developed countries who don't have UHC. We're also just about the only country involved in drug development, but UHC proponents never mention that. Other countries don't do much drug development because they *do* have UHC. A government administering health care will try to keep costs down, and one of the first things they'll do is cut back on pharma research. Bureaucrats who just don't understand the cost of R&D will cap the cost of XYZ to manufacture and delivery expense, plus a small profit.

If UHC cranks up in this country, you can expect drug development to die a sudden death. Whatever meds we have the day UHC becomes a reality may be all we'll ever get.

Additionally, when UHC is implemented, doctors' pay would be controlled by the government. From brain surgeon to a physician's assistant, they would get similar paychecks and those paychecks would probably be capped at a much lower level than any physicians currently earn.

The brain surgeon probably would have a bit more prestige than the PA, but not much more pay. He or she can't spend prestige. There'd be little fiscal incentive to spend another 10 years in med school. For that reason, whenever UHC comes up for discussion you'll hear many doctors talk about retirement or a change of occupation.

And finally, even patient care would be capped. For example, a 75-year-old needing knee replacement probably wouldn't get one; federal administrators would say expected life span makes the operation not cost effective; a knee replacement is supposed to last 20 years, but a 75-year-old might not be around that long; the government would want to spend knee-replacement money on a younger person in order to get more bang for their buck. An older person suffering from cancer could be told to take a Tylenol and attend end-of-life counseling, rather than receiving more aggressive treatment. Decisions like these would be in the hands of bureaucrats somewhere in Washington, not patients or doctors. The results are predictable.

Could euthanasia be far behind?

All things considered, UHC is a quantum leap backward. Health care in this country is expensive because it's worth it!

ON IMMIGRATION

We have an immigration problem in the United States, or more accurately an *illegal* immigration problem. The folks involved aren't really immigrants of any kind. They're trespassers who shouldn't be here at all, folks guilty of breaking and entering.

Broken Immigration System

Many people claim our immigration system is broken, that we need to fix or replace it. Maybe it is, but maybe it isn't. How could we know for sure since it's never been fully implemented? Calls for immigration reform from politicians are a ruse, smoke and mirrors to convince the gullible public that they're acting on the problem. But they probably wouldn't implement fully a new system either, resulting in another round of cries for immigration reform.

We don't seem to have much of a problem with our northern border, but thousands of people, a near continuous stream, overwhelm our border with Mexico. As if that isn't bad enough, we have no earthly idea who or how many of these people there are. Islamic jihadists could be in the mix—they'd blend in perfectly with our brown-skinned southern neighbors.

Our southern neighbors may not be all that chaste either. Members of the violent gang MS-13, for example, come from Mexico and points south. The gang has tens of thousands of members in the United States, a number that may be growing daily thanks to our porous southern border. MS-13 is involved in all manner of crime, from murder to drugs to robbery to prostitution. If there's illegal profit to be made, MS-13 has its fingers in the pie.

Aside from MS-13, there are members of other gangs and individual criminal "entrepreneurs" coming across our borders.

Separate the Good from the Bad
Proponents of open borders (amazingly, there are many such people) declare that people coming across our border are honest, hardworking folks just trying to make a living.

That may be true in most cases, but what about the other two, five, or 10 percent?

There was an e-mail note making the rounds that featured a picture of a bowl of M&Ms. The caption said, "This bowl contains 10,000 pieces of candy, but one percent of them are deadly poison. How many would you eat?"

That's a perfect analogy to what's going on at our southern border. We've got thousands of unknowns entering our country, many of them good people, but some of them are not. We should not allow unrestricted entry into our country, knowing that some of the folks coming in are bad. Even among the good ones, we need to be sure their numbers and the skills they bring don't exceed our needs. Because of all the illegals sneaking across the border, many educated, technically talented would-be immigrants have a longer wait to enter this country.

Instead, we need to use every means at our disposal to screen the folks coming here. We need would-be immigrants to fill out the requisite paperwork, allow time for us to scrutinize that paperwork, and then come here when their number is called. Even when they pass muster, there may be a waiting period. We can absorb only so many immigrants at a time.

Ceding that most of the folks coming across our southern border are good, honest people, that's not enough. We need to ensure that *all* people entering this country are good, honest people. We just can't take the chance that even a small percentage might be criminals or terrorists.

Open borders advocates tell us that we are a melting pot, that all our ancestors immigrated to this country, and that our friends below the border are no different.

Au contraire!

I'm a good one to speak to this since my dad immigrated to this country. Like most of the immigrants of the 1800s and early 1900s, he filled out the necessary paperwork, got on a ship, and came to this country. Once he arrived, he got in line with the other immigrants at Ellis Island to have his paperwork verified. When he had finished all the preliminaries, he found a job, learned the language, and assimilated. *That's* how it should be done.

Folks who come here illegally seldom do any of that stuff. They fill out no paperwork—okay, maybe for Welfare and food stamps. Many never learn the language and never consider assimilating. They live in barrios where everyone speaks Spanish exclusively. Some areas of cities like Miami have only Spanish street signs! Most of those folks have honest motives for wanting to be here, but legalization and assimilation aren't among them.

We concede that many of these folks come from poor areas where survival is tenuous and success out of reach. As much as we pity them and would like to help, we can't let everyone in those circumstances come here. Our priority must be to take care of our own citizens. Once we've done that, we can address the needs of others.

Sanctuary Cities

Many cities have declared they will not cooperate with Immigration and Customs Enforcement; when they have illegal aliens in custody, they refuse alert ICE before releasing them.

One of the more notorious results of this policy occurred in San Francisco. In 2015, Kate Steinle was killed by an illegal alien who'd been deported five times, but always sneaked back into the country. A jury found Garcia Zarate not guilty of murder but convicted him of illegal possession of a firearm, for which he received a three-year sentence. Three years for murder! The judge released Zarate on time already served, so he got nothing.

Zarate had been released from jail a few months before the murder, but the city didn't notify ICE that Zarate was even in custody. ICE had hoped to deport Zarate again and would have picked him up before he left jail; if they had, Steinle would still be alive. San Francisco takes the stance that deportation is a federal responsibility and the city wants no part of it, refuses to help in any way. In fact, the city has made it abundantly clear that illegal aliens are *welcome* in San Francisco.

The mayor of Oakland recently announced a pending ICE raid. Several hundred illegal aliens, mostly violent criminals were captured, but many more had already fled. Also, the heads-up provided by the mayor greatly increased the risk ICE agents faced since the suspects they planned to apprehend had been alerted and could have fought arrest.

There are many such examples that aren't quite as well known. In fact, my own grandson was murdered by an illegal alien who'd been released from jail only a few days earlier, again without notifying ICE. But that didn't modify my opinions on this problem whatever, it only cemented them.

In all such cases, sanctuary cities are putting the needs of illegal aliens above those of their own citizens. Sanctuary cities are saying in effect, *Illegal aliens are just trying to make a better life for themselves and we want to help, our citizens be damned!*

Some of the illegal aliens are good people, in fact most probably are, but the few bad apples can spoil the whole barrel. We need to vet thoroughly every person who comes into this country. We need to control the rate of entry for even the good, honest folks who want to come here. Every immigrant potentially takes a job away from a US citizen. Sanctuary cities allow illegal aliens unfettered access to our country imperiling the welfare and safety of our own citizens.

Looking out for our own citizens needs to be our priority.

Be Selective

Many folks south of the border are in dire straits, barely able to keep body and soul together, possibly at the mercy of cartels, coyotes, and corrupt officials. While we can sympathize, we can't solve everyone's problem.

"But, immigrants do the jobs that Americans just won't do," some would argue.

That's true up to a point: Immigrants do the jobs that Americans just won't do—for six bucks an hour. If there were no illegal immigrants, those same jobs would pay $12 or more an hour, and Americans would take them happily.

And don't be too concerned about the cost of vegetables or the cost to have your lawn mown. True, those prices would go up, but the cost of supporting illegal immigrants would go down. Illegal immigrants flood many of our schools, emergency rooms, and (unfortunately) prisons. That's a ton of support, some estimates are as high as a trillion dollars a year.

Prices up, support down. It'd be a wash, maybe a net gain.

Getting back to the Islamic terrorist threat, we have no idea how many have infiltrated our southern border. Apparently, officials are going to assume none of them have until one of them nukes Phoenix. Then they'll get serious about controlling immigration, but until then we're screwed.

Any immigrants allowed into this country must be encouraged to assimilate. The first step toward that goal must be: Learn the language. Not being able to converse is a major hurdle to getting along, getting ahead, and having a homogenous   country.

ON SOCIAL SECURITY

Social Security was a good idea in its time, but that time will be past soon. The annuitants are growing rapidly in number, to a point where the folks still contributing cannot sustain it. In other words, money going out will soon exceed money coming into the Treasury. The system will go bankrupt.

Some politicians claim that Social Security is in great shape. They're the same people who tell us the age at which annuitants can start drawing a check may need to be raised to 67 from 65. That's their way of admitting their first statement was untrue.

Another indication that Social Security is in bad shape is when those same politicians also tell us we may need to have means testing before an annuitant can begin receiving checks. In other words, if you're in good shape financially, they'll declare you don't need a Social Security check, or at least not a very big one. Means testing is just another way of delaying the inevitable, total collapse of the system by cheating donors out of their just due.

An analogy: Suppose Donald Trump went to his favorite haberdashery and picked out a new suit. After he had been fitted and paid the bill, the clerk would tell him to come back in a week for the final, tailored product. When he returned, the clerk wouldn't tell Trump, "You've already got 40 suits, so you don't need this one. You're not getting your money back either."

The same with Social Security. Donald Trump doesn't need a Social Security check, but that's his business. He paid for it, so he should get it. If he decides to donate the check to charity, that should be his choice, not the government's.

A Reasonable Replacement
Occasionally, a politician will suggest replacing Social Security with something else. Demagogues always come out of the woodwork, accusing proponents of trying to throw grandma out of the rest home and into the street. That's a complete distortion of the facts. Proponents for replacing Social Security always have a grandfather clause whereby SS annuitants would continue to get their monthly checks and, usually, folks who've been contributing for a long time would be allowed to stay in the old program if they didn't want to move to the new one.

What the proponents usually suggest is a privatized investment program. In 1986 the federal government did away with the old Civil Service Retirement System and implemented a new program called Federal Employees Retirement System. The heart of FERS is the Thrift Savings Plan, which allows employees to invest up to 10 percent of their salary in stocks, bonds, or the money market, with Uncle Sam matching part of those investments. Those TSP investments are tax-free, but upon retirement Uncle Sam would tax the withdrawals.

An employee could choose the fund in which his money would be invested. He'd get a simple, one-page monthly report showing how each fund had been doing and how much his investments had earned. If a different fund seemed to be doing better than the employee's current fund, the employee could divert his future investments to a different fund. On a quarterly basis, the employee could also transfer all previous investments into a different fund.

I was a federal employee at the time and had the option of staying in the old retirement system or transferring to the new one. I chose to stay in the old system, a mistake in retrospect. However, I had the option of putting money in the TSP as well as into the old system. I took that option for as much as they'd allow, which was five percent at the time (no matching government funds). In less than 10 years, my monthly earnings in the TSP account exceeded my gross salary!

See what I mean about not transferring to FERS being a mistake? I could have earned two or three times as much.

Under CSRS, the old retirement system, I contributed about the same amount as non-civil servants contributed to Social Security. The similarities end there. Depending on years of service, CSRS retirement could be as high as 80 percent of an annuitant's high three years' salary. FERS and TSP are even better than CSRS. Every civil servant I ever talked to thought TSP was the best thing the government ever did for us.

When implemented in 1935, Social Security was intended as a retirement supplement, not a stand-alone pension plan. Annuitants were never expected to subsist exclusively on Social Security income when they retired. Savings and other investments were supposed to be the main source of retirement income. TSP *would* provide a stand-alone retirement income.

Not everyone makes it to retirement age; some die before collecting their first check; others die soon thereafter. The bottom line is that some Social Security folks don't get to withdraw much if anything from their investments. Surviving spouses may get a reduced annuity, but adult children would get nothing in most cases. On the plus side, some folks live past retirement for decades, drawing Social Security. Those are the folks who truly benefit from the program.

Several politicians, including Bush the Younger, have advocated replacing Social Security with a TSP-like program. I'm not sure what the new program would have been called, but for purposes of this discussion we'll continue calling it TSP. Again, Social Security annuitants and long-time contributors would not have been affected, although folks who weren't retired might have been offered the option of converting to TSP. TSP would put people beginning their careers into a retirement program like the one Congress and other federal employees have.

There are major advantages of being in TSP, as opposed to Social Security. The rate of return is much better; choosing between stocks, bonds, and money market, one of those investments always will be on the rise. By checking the monthly TSP report and making easy changes, an investor would be sure to be in the right fund at the right time. A very conservative person might want to be in the money market; return on investment would be lousy (unless Jimmy Carter gets reelected), but it'd be an extremely safe investment, guaranteed never to lose money.

The government contracts with a private firm to manage TSP investments. In return for a small percentage (much less than one percent), that firm invests the money in very safe funds. The chances of TSP going under when, say, the Stock Market has a correction is infinitesimally small. TSP funds just aren't invested in volatile stocks, bonds, or money markets.

Whatever you've contributed and whatever those contributions have earned would always belong to you. Whenever you pass away, whatever is in that account would belong to your estate. If you pass away before retirement, you'd get no benefit from your investments, but your heirs certainly would.

So, why are some politicians so averse to a TSP-like program for everyone? After all, they're in one themselves and must know how good it is. What's good for the goose is apparently too good for the gander.

Those demagogues live on the backs of poor people. They claim to be for the little guy, when in fact they go out of their way to *create* more of them. They say they're standing up for the middle class, when everything they do, such as increasing taxes, drives the middle class closer to government dependency. If the little guys had a TSP-like retirement system, the demagogues would lose much of their constituency. The little guys would be pulling for Wall Street to do well, and that wouldn't bode well for the reelection chances of some politicians.

Maybe best of all, corrupt and inept politicians wouldn't be able to get their hands on the TSP funds, which wouldn't be in the Treasury; since 1965, they've been spending your Social Security contributions as fast as they come in.

ON BEING OFFENDED

There are plenty of things to be offended about without looking too hard. If someone rams your grocery cart or cuts you off in traffic, you rightfully could be offended. On the other hand, there are tons of things that just don't merit you getting your nose out of joint. I hope I'm preaching to the converted here, but there are some folks who are offended by almost anything.

Banning Christmas
This past Christmas season, someone put up a creche in his front yard. A neighbor in his subdivision complained to the homeowners' association, claiming to be offended, and they made the man take down his creche.

How devastated could the complainer have been by the presence of a creche? How sensitive could he be that a small building and some animal and human figures insulted him? Would it adversely have affected his life? What dire consequences did the presence of a creche threaten?

The complainer may have been the only person in the subdivision having a problem with the creche, yet he got his way. That's the polar opposite of democracy, a distinct minority ruling and that's not a good thing.

The HOA should have told the complainer to get over himself.

Many folks have bumper stickers that are offensive to others, but I've never heard of anyone being required to remove bumper stickers unless they were obscene. Maybe if those bumper stickers had a Christian message, someone probably would insist they be removed and authorities might agree.

You'll notice that I committed a major *faux pas* in the very first sentence of this section. In some circles it's offensive even to say "Christmas season" or anything of the sort. Some stores even train their clerks to say "Happy Holidays" so as not to offend anyone. I'm offended by that! I often go out of my way to greet those clerks with a "Merry Christmas" and often get a knowing smile and a subdued similar response.

Many stores, schools, and other institutions observe Winter Break, Holiday Season, or some other innocuous term to describe events occurring in late December. One of these days the complainers will try to prevent calendar makers from using the word Christmas on their wares.

The offended often point to the First Amendment as preventing the establishment of a religion. They think everyone, especially government organizations, should be totally secular. They might be okay with you praying in your own home, behind closed doors, but the offended don't want to hear or observe it.

To quote the relevant part of the First Amendment: "Congress shall make no law respecting an establishment of religion, *or prohibiting the free exercise thereof.*" The offended never seem to mention the italicized part. The display of a creche should be considered a "free exercise thereof." Such things as displaying a creche or wishing others a Merry Christmas are also guaranteed by the First Amendment.

The First Amendment guarantees freedom *of* religion, not freedom *from* religion.

In God We Trust

Many folks believe we should take all references to a Higher Being out of the public sector. For example, they say we should delete "Under God" from the Pledge of Allegiance, take the word "God" off our currency, and remove the Ten Commandments from courthouses and such.

Those folks may be living in the wrong country. The religious icons and references currently in public use have been around long before it became *de rigueur* to remove them. The United States was founded on Judeo-Christian values, such as the Ten Commandments. Those offended seem bent on eliminating anything remotely religious. As bad as that is, the worse thing is that some people in authority support their complaints.

Race Offenses

Some blacks call each other "nigger" as a term of affection. White folks, however, are allowed no such latitude. I get that. That racial epithet is not normally used by white folks as a term of affection and shouldn't be condoned.

On the other hand, some blacks are offended by nearly anything a white person says about them, even if it's an undisputed truth. For example, I'd expect to be ostracized by some in the black community if I pointed out that blacks commit more than their share of crime or that blacks have an unacceptably high rate of out-of-wedlock births. While that's all true, it just isn't PC to say so.

Jimmy "The Greek" Snyder lost his NFL analyst's job because he said blacks on average are bigger, stronger, and more athletic than whites because they were bred to be that way in the days of slavery. Slave owners bought big, strong slaves and that resulted in big strong slave offspring. Jimmy was right and no one contested it, but he got fired anyway. Folks just aren't supposed to state the truth if it somehow puts blacks in a bad light. Seems to me the slave owners are the ones shown in a bad light.

Those examples are fairly clear-cut, but there are a few race hustlers of various colors in this country who bend over backward to be racially offended. If you said, "Good morning" to them, they'd be offended. Whenever there's an incident of some sort involving a black who might be the victim of a crime, you can count of at least one of these race hustlers to hop a jet and get to the scene in time to exacerbate the situation. These hustlers are often proven wrong about the victim they're defending, but that doesn't elicit an apology or even a comment from them.

I'm wracking my brain but can't think of a single incident where one of these race hustlers contributed to a solution. Rather, they whip the neighborhood into a riotous frenzy often resulting in looting and arson. A competent sheriff should meet such a troublemaker as he gets off the plane and issue an ultimatum: "Get back on the plane and get out of town. Otherwise, I'm putting you in jail. If you choose the latter, you will not be allowed to talk to the press until after you leave town."

That last statement is the key: These people are in town for publicity, which results in monetary contributions.

They're in it for the money, the black community and everyone else be damned.

ON VETERANS

We owe quite a bit to quite a few people. For example, we have doctors who look after our health, policemen who look after our safety, and clergy who look after our spiritual needs. Another group I'm going to spotlight is our military, especially military veterans.

Public Response

When our soldiers, sailors, and airmen came home from WWII, they couldn't walk into a bar and buy a drink. Their drinks were always on the house or on the tab of a grateful patron. Following the Korean War, vets could walk into a bar and buy their own drinks; fellow patrons mostly left them alone. But when a Vietnam vet walked into a bar, he was liable to get thrown out or have a patron pick a fight with him.

I feel badly for the 'Nam vets and the way some of them were treated. In most cases, they were conscripted, serving their country because they had to. Few of them knew what the war was about; they were just following orders. Yet, many civilians, who also knew little about the war, chose to spit on the vets, call them names, and do all they could to express their outrage. Some vets were called "baby killers," when they were quite the opposite.

Most 'Nam vets rolled with the punches and didn't react, but darned if I can see how they did it. Some of the abuse heaped on them was atrocious.

Since 'Nam, civilians are pretty much back on an equal footing with more recent combat vets. Civilians might not buy drinks, but they won't pick fights with them either.

Take a Minute

I often see gentlemen and occasionally ladies wearing a cap or coat declaring their military service. I'm glad to see they're proud enough to declare it openly—they should be. They made tremendous sacrifices and often braved great dangers, all to protect and preserve peace and freedom for the rest of us.

When I see a veteran, if I can do so without being intrusive, I go up to him, shake his hand, and tell him how much I appreciate his service to our country. That almost always brings a big smile and then *they thank me!*

When I tell a vet how much I appreciate everything he's done, he'll invariably say, "I just followed orders."

With all due respect, that just can't be true. Yes, they did follow orders, but there often was no superior around to give those orders. Consequently, the vet was on his own to improvise or implement his own plan. A maxim of war: "The best war plan ever devised is absolutely useless 10 minutes after the first shot is fired." That's the situation in which many of our vets found themselves. They didn't just follow orders, they made their own.

Occasionally I'll run across a vet who apologetically admits he was *only* in the Reserves or National Guard. I don't accept such modesty. Anyone who wore a uniform, no matter where or for how long, is a full-fledged veteran and deserves our eternal gratitude.

I'd swear some of those veterans practically levitate as I leave them. They've done so much for me it makes me glad to see them glad.

If you see a vet, consider telling him (or her) how much you appreciate his service. He'll be glad you did and so will you.

If his wife/girlfriend happens to be with him, tell her, "You picked a winner, ma'am."

She'll probably reply, "You bet I did!"

HonorAir

Not long after the WWII Memorial opened in 2004, a private pilot in Ohio began flying veterans to Washington DC to see their memorial. That effort quickly expanded to become a national project. I had the distinct honor and privilege to serve as a guardian (chaperone, escort) on one of those flights. Here's a recap of our schedule that day:

- Leave Asheville, NC, airport at 7 am
- Arrive Washington's Reagan-National Airport at 8:30
- Tour the WWII Memorial from 9-11
- Box lunch aboard buses as we tour the city from 11-1
- Visit Vietnam War and Lincoln Memorials from 1-2
- Visit Korean War Memorial from 2-3
- Tour Arlington National Cemetery and Marine Memorial from 3-4
- Tour Women's War Memorial from 4-5

- Depart Reagan-National 5:30
- Arrive Asheville 7 pm

The veterans had a huge day. Smiles were prevalent and tear-stained faces were very common. It seemed there was a moving moment nearly every second of the day, among them:

- Before departing Asheville, all vets were given special jackets and caps
- We were served a hot breakfast on the flight to Washington DC
- Firetrucks shot plumes of water over our plane as we traversed the DC tarmac
- A band and chorus from West Point performed patriotic songs as we entered the terminal
- Senator Bob Dole and his wife Libby met us at the entrance to the WWII Memorial
- North Carolina Representatives and Senators were also on hand
- At the end of the day at Reagan-National, a band played '40s music and girls wearing period attire danced to songs like *Boogie-Woogie Bugle Boy of*

Company B—one spry vet jitterbugged with one of the girls
- On the flight home, Mail Call was announced, just as happened during the war
- Vets were given "mail" secretly created by relatives and friends for this special moment
- As we deplaned in Asheville, we were greeted by thousands of cheering people lining the airport corridors from the gate all the way to the parking lot

The three vets for whom I served as guardian have since passed away, but I'm so happy they got to see their memorial and be spoiled rotten for a day. Lord knows they deserved it.

There aren't too many WWII vets still with us, but the project continues. Any remaining WWII vets are more than welcome to go on future Honor Flights (new name, same organization), but these flights now include vets from Korea, Vietnam, Desert Storm, and any other campaigns in which our country has been involved. If you or someone you know would like to go on one of these flights, please do so. It costs absolutely nothing!

For information go to:

https://www.honorflight.org/veteran-application/

ON MUSIC

Not everyone has the same taste in music, and that's fine. I'm a classical guy but wasn't always one. My early exposure to the genre wasn't good. I'm not sure if I just heard some bad examples or if my musical palate had yet to develop.

All my grade school and high school friends were into pop music, so I gravitated in that direction, too. I stayed there until the Beatles and Rolling Stones arrived. I tried my best to like their songs, but the British Invasion was the death of pop music for me.

Tuning through the AM dial one day (we're talking about the Roaring BCs here, the late 1960s), I ran across songs by Jerry Lee Lewis and Conway Twitty, guys I had enjoyed hearing on pop stations. Their music and that of several other former pop artists could now be heard on country stations, so that's where I moved my allegiance and that's where it stayed for 25 years.

My wife and I went to the movies one day, around 1993. We saw *The Shawshank Redemption*, a film based on a Stephen King book. It was a good movie about a guy convicted to life in prison for murdering his wife—the movie never made it clear whether the protagonist was guilty. The prison warden and guards were cruel, sadistic fellows not above beating or even killing inmates. The protagonist had been a banker and endeared himself to those thugs by managing their investments and doing their taxes. In return, the thugs gave him protection from other inmates and a cushy job as the prison librarian.

One day, the protagonist got crosswise with the warden and locked himself in the warden's office. There he played a record over the prison PA system, an Italian opera aria.

I had no idea what those divas were saying but knew singing talent and beautiful music when I heard it. I decided that having that song would be a good addition to my CD collection. We sat through the movie credits and learned the aria came from Mozart's *Marriage of Figaro*. The first chance I got I went to a record store to find such a CD. Unfortunately, I found about a dozen renditions of *Figaro*. Logic decreed that some of those discs probably were superb, but a few others might sound like a jug band recorded in someone's garage. Not knowing which was which, I left the store without making a purchase.

Weeks later in another store, I noticed a table of remaindered books titled *How to Build a Classical Music Library*. The book seemed like a probable guide to learn which versions of *Figaro* were good and which weren't. The price was right, so I bought copy and used it as a guide toward the purchase of my first classical CD, and with good results. From there, I used the book to build the beginnings of my classical collection.

Looking back to my early days of pop music, I should have realized I might be a classical guy. I gravitated toward instrumentals by folks like Henry Mancini. My classical collection is almost exclusively instrumental, not much in the way of vocals at all.

Classical music, the instrumental stuff anyway, is great background for dining, conversations, and reading. Don't try that with the Stones!

It seems the worse the music, the louder it must be played for maximum enjoyment. You never hear a car on the street blasting a Beethoven quartet; instead it's always heavy metal, rap, or some such.

If you're a classical person, you probably agree with that assessment. If not, maybe you just haven't been exposed to the right kind of classical music.

There are many varieties of classical music. I have friends who like Russian music, enjoying the anger evident in some of it. I know other people who enjoy the spicy dissonance of modern classical music. If either of those is your thing, you may not like my kind of classical music. I'm more into smooth, melodic stuff; I'm not interested in music that sounds like it was written the day the composer's dog died or the day his wife wrecked the car.

If you agree with my views so far but haven't acquired a taste for classical music yet, here are some places to start, depending on what you think you might like (in no particular order).

If you like piano music, you might try:

1. Any of Mozart's concertos
2. Any of Beethoven's concertos
3. Mozart's *Piano Duets*
4. Clemente's *Piano Duets*
5. Chopin's *Piano Waltzes*

6. Any of Schubert's sonatas

If you like string music, you might try:

1. Any of Mozart's violin concertos (especially #3)
2. Beethoven's *Violin Concerto*
3. Dvorak's *Cello Concerto*
4. Tchaikovsky's *Serenade for Strings*
5. Vivaldi's *The Four Seasons* (maybe the best string composition ever)

If you like woodwind music, you might try:

1. Any of Albinoni's oboe concertos
2. Mozart's *Clarinet Concerto*
3. Mozart's *Clarinet Quintet* (his valedictory composition)
4. Mozart's *Oboe Concerto*

If you like brass music, you might try:

1. Haydn's *Trumpet Concerto*
2. Any of Mozart's horn concertos
3. Telemann's *Trumpet Concerto*

If you like orchestral music, you might try:

1. Any of Haydn's symphonies
2. Any of Mozart's symphonies
3. Bach's *Orchestral Suites*
4. Handel's *Music for the Royal Fireworks*

5. Handel's *Water Music*
6. Highlights from any of Tchaikovsky's ballets
7. Mendelssohn's *Fourth Symphony*
8. Ravel's *Bolero*

For choral music, here are some of the best:

1. Beethoven's *Ninth Symphony*
2. Handel's *Messiah* (highlights)
3. Mozart's *Marriage of Figaro* (highlights)
4. Nana Mouskouri's *Classical* (CD)
5. *The #1 Opera Album*, the best recordings of 40 favorite arias

And finally, if you're planning a dinner party where some soft, soothing instrumental music would be a wonderful background, look no further than Mozart's *Adagios*. It's a two-CD set containing about two-and-a-half hours of some of the best slow movements in classical music. Mozart wrote some of the most mellow music in history. If you can't relax listening to this stuff, you may need prescription drugs!

ON BOOKS

For several years I wrote book reviews for *Prime Times*, a regional publication in western North Carolina. In every issue I reviewed the best book of the 10 or 12 I had read the previous month. Most of us can't wait to tell others about a good book we've just finished. That's me for sure, so that reviewing gig was right up my alley. Sadly, the magazine went out of business, probably because they were publishing my stuff.

Just kidding…I hope.

I still read quite a bit, both fiction and nonfiction. In my old age, I don't have the time or patience to finish a book that doesn't grab me. That doesn't happen too often because I've developed some guidelines to weed out the not-so-good books. I'll share those guidelines with you here:

1. Don't pay any attention to book cover blurbs, at least not those by other authors. Those people are paid to praise a book, but probably haven't read a word of it. Or else authors trade reviews with each other, quid pro quo.

2. Reviews from newspapers and magazines are much more reliable.
3. Another good barometer is Kirkus Reviews. They are paid by the author or publisher to review a book, but they don't pull any punches.
4. A book winning a Pulitzer Prize is a very good bet, a Nobel Prize not so much.
5. Word of mouth from other readers can be a good guide.
6. Check actual reader reviews at a website such as Amazon; if there are a significant number of reviews, four stars is very good and four-and-a-half is excellent.

Since you've gotten this far, you must like to read so I'm going to make some recommendations. In no particular order:

Fiction:

1. *Robert Lewis Taylor's *The Travels of Jaimie McPheeters*, the hilarious adventures of a young boy in the old West.
2. *John Kennedy *Toole's A Confederacy of Dunces*, a mama's boy and a plethora of other seemingly unrelated characters eventually merge in a comical conclusion.
3. *McKinley Kantor's *Andersonville*, an epic novel about the notorious Confederate prison camp in

Georgia.

4. Ayn Rand's *Atlas Shrugged*, a sprawling allegory illustrating the author's objectivism philosophy.

5. Joe Gores' *32 Cadillacs*, the story of a swindle that puts *The Sting* in the shade.

6. Joseph Heller's *Catch 22*, biting satire about WWII

7. Joseph Heller's *God Knows*, the wry "autobiography" of King David provides a smile per paragraph and a chuckle per page

8. Tim Dorsey's series about a serial killer and his stoner buddy frolicking all over Florida righting wrongs

*Pulitzer Prize winner

Non-Fiction:

1. Bill Bryson's *A Short History of Nearly Everything*, a folksy but surprisingly intellectual explanation of a wide variety of topics, including astrophysics and Darwinism

2. Audie Murphy's *To Hell and Back*, an autobiography of WWII's most decorated soldier, later a movie star

3. Hugh Shelton's *Without Hesitation*, the memoirs of a former Chairman of the Joint Chiefs of Staff

4. Albert Einstein's *Relativity*, an easy read straight from the horse's mouth

5. Richard Feynman's, *Surely You're Joking, Mr. Feynman*, the memoirs of a wry Nobel Prize-winning

physicist involved in everything from building the A-bomb to solving the space shuttle Challenger disaster

6. *David McCullough's *Truman*, a biography of Harry S. Truman

7. Allan Barra's *Yogi Berra*, a great biography of the beloved Yankee catcher

8. Ben Bradlee's *The Kid*, a warts-and-all biography of Ted Williams

9. Marty Appel's *Casey Stengel*, a biography of one of MLBs more successful managers, also one of its better early players

10. Peter Golenbock's *Dynasty*, the history of the New York Yankees of 1949-1964

11. Alex Karras, *Even Big Guys Cry*, the autobiography of the defensive lineman to whom Jimmy "The Greek" Snyder assigned the most points ever when handicapping an NFL game

12. Jane Leavy's *The Last Boy*, the definitive biography of Mickey Mantle

13. Maynard Solomon's *Mozart*, a biography of classical music's most eccentric genius

14. John Linder and Neil Boortz' *The Fair Tax Book*, eliminating the IRS with a tax system that would be simple and fair to everyone

15. **Adam Makos and Larry Alexander's *A Higher Call*, the account of a WWII German fighter pilot who

escorted a crippled American bomber out of enemy ter-
ritory

*Pulitzer Prize winner
**Should have won a Pulitzer

EPILOGUE

Thank you for reading *Philosophies and Profundities*. If you've made it this far, you must have enjoyed it. I hope so. Maybe some of my observations have brought you around to a different way of thinking. Or maybe you're more convinced than ever that your opposing views are valid. In any event, civil discourse is always enlightening, if only to learn how someone else thinks.

About the Author

Ed Nielsen is retired, following a career as a civilian employee of the Department of Defense. He has published hundreds of newspaper and magazine articles, as well as seven other books. For more information, go to:

BooksByEdNielsen.com.

He and his wife Connie live in Hendersonville, North Carolina, where he spends his spare time on the three Rs (reading, writing, and running).

www.ingramcontent.com/pod-product-compliance
Lightning Source LLC
Chambersburg PA
CBHW051744250726
48659CB00001B/236